I0560759

As a media producer and consultant, I work with pastors and church leaders daily, helping them use media to engage today's culture more effectively. That work is incredibly inspiring, but at the same time, I'm seeing more pastors than ever leave the ministry entirely. That's why I was so thrilled to see Dean Taylor's new book, *The Healthy Pastor: Stewarding Your Personal Life for Long-Term Ministry*. Pastor burnout is real, and it's destroying our effective witness to the world. If you're a pastor or ministry leader of any kind, consider this preventive medicine. The principles in this book can change the direction of your life and potentially thousands of lives you touch.

–Phil Cooke

  Author, Co-Founder and CEO of Cooke Media Group, Los Angeles, California

The Healthy Pastor is a treasure that has the smell of sheep on every page. It is written by a seasoned shepherd whose track record of leading with "skillful hands" and "integrity of heart" is etched across several decades (Ps 78:72). I've known Dean through all his years of ministry and training. His humble pastoral walk has left me with faithful and humble footprints to follow. The ground he covers in this volume is simply astounding. It reads like what it is— Dean's own journal of reflections and research from his decades of local church love and stewardship. No stone has remained unturned, even the jagged rocks that we pastors want to ignore. I wholeheartedly recommend this volume to men considering pastoral ministry, training for ministry, entering the ministry, enduring the ministry, and approaching the sunset of ministry. We are in Dean's debt for his *shepherding the shepherds* with these words of grace.

–Jim Newcomer

  Senior Pastor, Calvary Baptist Church, Ypsilanti, Michigan; Adjunct Biblical Counseling Professor

Ministry is a calling, but it can also be a heavy burden. *The Healthy Pastor* is a must-read for every pastor seeking to lead with wisdom, endurance, and spiritual vitality. In a time when burnout and exhaustion threaten many in ministry, this book provides a refreshing and practical guide to maintaining physical, emotional, and spiritual well-being. With wisdom, honesty, and deep biblical insight, Dean Taylor offers practical guidance for maintaining a vibrant faith. Whether you're a seasoned leader or just starting in ministry, this book will challenge and encourage you to pursue a life of balance and faithfulness. I highly recommend it!

—Michael Blackstone

Businessman

Dean Taylor understands the blessings and challenges of pastoral ministry. In *The Healthy Pastor*, he comes alongside fellow pastors to offer encouragement and practical advice. Personally, this book, although convicting at times, inspired me to keep running the race with endurance and joy. I love how Dean draws from his deep knowledge of Scripture and vast experience to offer wise counsel that will help any pastor navigate the unique challenges of his calling. Each chapter's practical action steps and personal evaluation questions significantly helped me. I plan to read this book again with the elders in my church and gift it to future pastors as a trusted resource for their long-term effectiveness.

—Kevin Williams

Senior Pastor, Meadowlands Baptist Church, AB, Canada

Reading *The Healthy Pastor* was like taking a breath of fresh air. It gave me hope for men who struggle, men who are stressed, and men who are mentoring others for ministry. I entered the ministry at a time when the trend was that ministry was a sacrifice, and I received little instruction on the concept of stewardship. I saw the cost of this firsthand. Many men lost their wives, children, health, and reputation (doctrinal and moral failure). Men left the ministry disillusioned. Dean similarly describes the *"ecclesiastical crisis"* as a result of the *"current dearth of available men"* combined with *"the number of pastors leaving the ministry."* Pastors and wives tell him, *"No one is discussing this problem."*

Dean is God's man for this hour. His book should be mandatory reading for any man aspiring to pastoral ministry. With a personal mission to be a *"friend to men in ministry,"* Dean speaks with rare and relevant insight into the life and ministry of a pastor. While rooted in Scripture and diligent research, his writing is rich in personal illustrations from years of pastoral ministry and a heart of genuine concern and compassion for churches and pastors. This book will be clarifying (self-care vs. self-centeredness), compelling, convicting, comforting, and Christ-centered. I highly recommend this book. Deacons should read *The Healthy Pastor!* Read it. Share it. Give it to others in ministry. Healthy churches need healthy pastors.

—Tim Capon
State Representative, Iowa Association of Regular Baptist Churches

As pastors, we are wise to have periodic physical checkups and, in the same vein, pastoral ministry checkups. Sadly, just as we are reluctant to admit a physical need and seek help, we are prone to do the same in pastoral ministry. I have counseled many pastors over the years and served as a senior pastor for forty years. I can say *The Healthy Pastor* addresses the heart issues that produce unhealthy pastors and, therefore, unhealthy churches. Dean's journey in ministry, his mentors, and his educational background enable him to give a cutting-edge diagnosis and remedy that will help pastors be restored to ministry health.

—Dale Cunningham
Associate Pastor, Boones Creek Bible Church; Leader and Founder of D&D Ministries

The Healthy Pastor lifts the rug on a ministry subject that has been swept under it for quite some time. It repeatedly forced me to stop, think, and process. These are signs of a good book! It encouraged thoughts I already had and stimulated thoughts I had never considered. If you are in the ministry, read this book. If you know someone in the ministry, read this book.

—J. Mark Kittrell
President, Pacific Rim Missions International

Sheep without a shepherd are in danger of wandering away, going hungry, and being attacked. As a camp director for over four decades, I have served our Lord as a sheepdog, pushing the teenage sheep back to their shepherds (pastors) for year-round growth and protection. Dean Taylor shares his experience as a pastor and a professor, emphasizing the essential truths needed to encourage young men to consider pastoral ministry. A healthy pastor is motivated by both a personal love for his Lord, the Chief Shepherd, and a genuine love for the sheep God calls him to lead—an excellent read for pastors, young and old alike.

–Rand Hummel
　　Author; Staff Evangelist, the Wilds Christian Association

This is the book that I, as a pastor for thirty-nine years, should have read in the early part of my life and ministry. Now that I have the privilege of reading *The Healthy Pastor*, without reservation and with complete confidence, I highly recommend Dr. Dean Taylor's work to my fellow ministers, especially Filipino pastors. Reading this book will definitely revolutionize the life and ministry of a man called a "shepherd after God's own heart."

–Jun D. Oguilla
　　Pastor, Maranatha Baptist Church, Villamonte, Bacolod City, Philippines

THE HEALTHY PASTOR

**Stewarding Your Personal Life
for Long-Term Ministry**

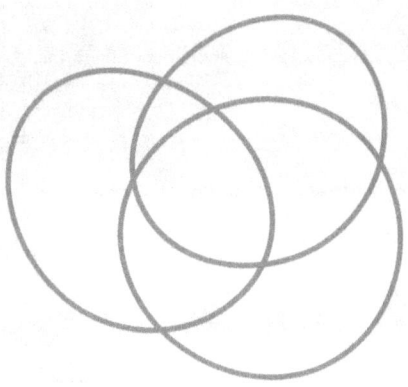

DEAN H. TAYLOR

FAITH PUBLICATIONS
ANKENY, IOWA

The Healthy Pastor
©2025 by Dean H. Taylor

No part of this publication may be reproduced, distributed, or transmitted in any form or by any means, including electronic or mechanical methods, except for brief quotations in reviews and other noncommercial uses permitted by copyright law, without the prior written permission of Faith Publications.

Unless otherwise indicated, all Scripture quotations are taken from the Holy Bible, English Standard Version® (ESV®), copyright © 2001 by Crossway, a publishing ministry of Good News Publishers. Used by permission. All rights reserved.

Scripture quotations marked (AMP) are taken from *The Amplified Bible* ®, copyright © 1954, 1958, 1962, 1964, 1965, 1987 by The Lockman Foundation. Used by permission (www.Lockman.org) All rights reserved.

Scripture quotations marked (CSB) have been taken from the Christian Standard Bible®, copyright © 2017 by Holman Bible Publishers. Used by permission. Christian Standard Bible® and CSB® are federally registered trademarks of Holman Bible Publishers.

Scripture quotations marked (NASB) are taken from the New American Standard Bible®, copyright © 1960, 1962, 1963, 1968, 1971, 1972, 1973, 1975, 1977, 1995 by The Lockman Foundation. Used by permission.

Scripture quotations and/or notes quoted by permission. Quotations designated (NET) are from the NET Bible®, copyright © 1996–2006 by Biblical Studies Press, L.L.C. All rights reserved.

Scripture quotations marked (NKJV) are taken from the New King James Version®, copyright © 1982 by Thomas Nelson. Used by permission. All rights reserved.

Scripture quotations marked (NIV) are taken from the Holy Bible, New International Version®, NIV®. Copyright © 1973, 1978, 1984, 2011 by Biblica, Inc.™ Used by permission of Zondervan. All rights reserved worldwide. www.zondervan.com. The "NIV" and "New International Version" are trademarks registered in the United States Patent and Trademark Office by Biblica, Inc.™

Scripture quotations marked (YLT) are taken from the 1898 Young's Literal Translation of the Holy Bible by J.N. Young, (author of the *Young's Analytical Concordance*), public domain.

All words in bold in Scripture passages are the emphasis of the author.

The Secret Place by Cheryl Reid and Ron Hamilton. Copyright © 2006 by Majesty Music, Inc. All rights reserved; used by permission.

Designed by Lance Young with Higher Rock Creative Studio

ISBN 978-1-960820-10-5 (hardcover)
ISBN 978-1-960820-09-9 (paperback)
ISBN 978-1-960820-11-2 (digital)

Library of Congress Control Number: 2025905195

Faith Publications
1900 NW 4th St.
Ankeny, IA 50023
Faith.edu/publications

Printed in the United States of America
All rights reserved

15   14   13   12   11   10   9   8   7   6   5   4   3   2   1

WITH DEEP
APPRECIATION TO

Dr. Robert Taylor

Pastor Emeritus, Colonial Hills Baptist Church, Indianapolis
who models healthy balance in his personal life and pastoral work
in ways that have shaped me for a lifetime of ministry

TABLE OF

CONTENTS

Part 1—Starting Point
1 The Need for Healthy Pastors 3
2 The Biblical Basis and Definition of a Healthy Pastor 11

Part 2—Foundational Principles
3 A Healthy Pastor's Source of Identity 19
4 Self-Care as Stewardship 31
5 Guarding Integrity for a Persevering Ministry 43

Part 3—Critical Areas
6 A Pastor's Antidote for Unworthiness 55
7 Ministry Stress Relief 63
8 Action Steps for Overcoming Discouragement 75
9 Overpowering Ministry Disappointments with Kingdom Hope 95
10 The Antidote for Comparison 107
11 Understanding Compassion Fatigue 113

Part 4—Essential Practices
12 Communion with God 125
13 Companionship in a Ministry Marriage 135
14 Taking a Personal Retreat 151
15 Controlling Your Time 157
16 Holy Distractions 169
17 Disciplined Physical Habits 183
18 Holy Companions 189

Part 5—Recovery and Final Prayer
19 Basic Actions for Recovering Personal Health 201
20 My Prayer for You 205

ACKNOWLEDGMENTS

When I transitioned from pastoring to teaching, I adopted a personal mission that includes being a friend to men in ministry. Mature men helped me through my own challenges and growth as a pastor, and I aspire to be the same kind of friend to others. I thank those who have invested in me, as well as pastors who have invited me into their lives, giving me the opportunity to bear their burdens with them. My goal for this book is to provide further encouragement to my brothers in ministry.

The catalyst for studying this topic was an invitation from Pastor Tim Capon, State Representative of the Iowa Association of Regular Baptist Churches, to present a workshop on "The Healthy Pastor." More opportunities in various settings opened to address issues pastors face in their personal lives. My passion to write on it grew, and here we are.

I enlisted Dr. Dan Brown, Professor of Practical Theology at Faith Baptist Theological Seminary, and Pastor Stephen Moore, Lead Pastor of Ballard Creek Church, to read through the manuscript. Each provided input that I implemented. I read chapters to my undergraduate Pastoral Studies students and seminary Doctor of Ministry students in a writer's workshop format which resulted in additional refinements.

Dr. Tim Little, Director of Faith Publications at Faith Baptist Bible College and Theological Seminary, encourages me to write, shepherds projects through the process, and makes sure all the details of publishing a book are handled with integrity, professionalism, and excellence. Dr.

Little's passion for our faculty to write is opening a new era of publishing for Faith Baptist Bible College and Theological Seminary and expanding its realm of influence.

Proofreading by Dr. Joshua Boyd, Chair of General Education at Faith Baptist Bible College, ensures clarity and correctness of content. I'm thankful for Dr. Boyd's eyes on this project.

Nancy Lohr's ministry heart and editing expertise transform a manuscript into a publishable work. Nancy edited my first book, *The Thriving Church*. When she retired as Acquisitions Editor of JourneyForth Books, I thought I had missed the opportunity to involve her in this project. However, she graciously agreed to take it on. I am so glad, and you will be too!

Ironically, I began researching *The Healthy Pastor* in earnest while recovering from the second of two shoulder surgeries. Both resulted from cycling accidents and involved significant pain and months-long recovery, requiring great degrees of sympathy and care from my wife. She informed me if it happens a third time, I'm on my own. Otherwise, she has been very supportive of my pursuits. Faith never ceases to encourage my writing efforts, patiently listens to my developing ideas, always provides a practical and wise perspective, and is my steadfast companion in love, family, fun, life, and ministry.

STARTING POINT

CHAPTER ONE

THE NEED
FOR HEALTHY PASTORS

WE NEED THIS

A few years ago, I was asked to present a workshop on what it means to be a healthy pastor. That was the catalyst to investigate a topic I had not really studied before. I wanted to learn more, so I started researching, writing, and presenting more workshops. I often hear from both pastors and wives, "No one is talking about this. We need this."

I'm not the only one addressing the subject, but it's true that pastors aren't encouraged enough to pay attention to their personal health. It's also possible pastors aren't taking action on what they hear.

What does the term "healthy pastor" bring to your mind? A physically fit pastor who runs 5Ks and half-marathons? A slim and trim pastor who has no problem buttoning his sport coat? A pastor who takes problems and challenges in stride while always appearing calm and unstressed? Possibly you associate it with the false prosperity teaching that guarantees physical and material abundance.

We need to have a right perspective on what it means to be a healthy pastor. In this chapter we'll establish the need for talking about it, and in the next chapter we will discern the biblical basis and provide a definition for the healthy pastor.

Why are we even talking about pastors being healthy? Let me give you some reasons for focusing on this topic.

EIGHT ARGUMENTS

Pastors are burning out, bailing out, and crashing out.

You are likely aware of the event when terrorists flew airplanes into the Twin Towers in New York and the Pentagon in Washington, D.C. on September 11, 2001. Now known simply as 9/11, this event had a life-altering effect on US citizens for decades afterward.

In a similar way, the COVID-19 pandemic significantly impacted pastors and churches. 2020–21 was an extremely stressful time to be a pastor. "The Great Resignation" was one effect of the pandemic in which many employees decided they didn't want to go to work any longer, so they quit. This trend affected pastors as well. Many decided to quit the ministry, resulting in "The Great Pastor Resignation."

Consider this stunning report: as of March 2022, 42 percent of pastors have seriously considered leaving, not just their churches, but the ministry altogether. Three main factors cited are the immense stress of the job (56 percent), feeling lonely and frustrated (43 percent), and political division affecting their churches (38 percent).[1] At least two of these factors can be considered issues of personal health. Also, pastors who haven't considered quitting are still challenged by these issues.[2]

In addition to burning out and bailing out, we all know of pastors who have crashed out, having to leave the ministry because of moral or ethical failure. The frequency and devastation of these occurrences necessitates that every pastor give careful attention to his personal life.

---

1. "Pastors Share Top Reasons They've Considered Quitting Ministry in the Past Year," Barna.com, https://www.barna.com/research/pastors-quitting-ministry.

2. Ibid.

Pastors are characteristically unhealthy.

A study from October 2021 indicates that "only one in three pastors is considered 'healthy' in terms of well-being." The assessment of "healthy" is based on those who score themselves "good" in categories of "relational, spiritual, physical, emotional, vocational, [and] financial" well-being. Only 35 percent meet this criterion according to their own self-assessment. This is a factor in those who are considering quitting; they are "less healthy in the well-being categories compared to pastors who are not considering giving up full-time ministry."[3]

Of those who have considered quitting, many say their spiritual formation (Bible reading, prayer, and personal worship) has taken a back seat to pastoral duties. Only one in ten agree they prioritize self-care as a pastor.[4]

Pastoral ministry is a stress-inducing vocation that can have negative effects on your personal health.

I don't have to prove this to you, but it might help you to know it is documented by the *Journal of Pastoral Care & Counseling* in a study called "Health Effects of a Religious Vocation." According to this study, the responsibilities of leading worship services, preparing and delivering sermons, serving as the spiritual and administrative leader of a religious organization, overseeing and officiating at weddings and funerals, visiting ill and homebound congregants, counseling, and developing and enacting organizational policies "culminates in inordinate demands on the time and energy of clergy, with 25 percent of clergy reporting they spend over sixty hours per week in ministry-related duties."[5]

---

3. "38 percent of U.S. Pastors Have Thought About Quitting Full-Time Ministry in the Past Year," Barna.com, https://www.barna.com/research/pastors-well-being.

4. "For Pastors Who Want to Quit, Self-Care & Soul-Care Slip," Barna.com, https://www.barna.com/research/spiritual-formation-back-seat.

5. Benjamin Webb, "Health Effects of a Religious Vocation: Perspectives from Christian and Jewish Clergy," *Journal of Pastoral Care and Counseling*, 70(4), 266–271, https://doi.org/10.1177/1542305016672669 .

It's not only the amount of time, but the kind of work that pastors engage in during those hours that produces stress. And the result is not pretty. Although clergy have lower mortality rates than the general population, their susceptibility to death from heart disease, often stress related, is among the highest. Clergy are "disproportionately affected by obesity" and are prone to mental health problems such as depression, anxiety, and bipolar disorder. Pastors have a hard time maintaining boundaries between work and family life, find it difficult to discuss their struggles with others, and often face conflict with church members. These pressures on a pastor often contribute to burnout.

The article concludes, "The myriad responsibilities of clergy, routine or otherwise, reveal an occupation where the risk for negative health outcomes is endemic. In addition to providing coping resources for clergy, it is clear that preventative measures should be considered as a strategy for improving health outcomes among clergy."[6]

In other words, ministry is inherently stressful and can erode personal health. A pastor needs to be proactive in cultivating and protecting his personal health in order to sustain long-term ministry.

The criteria for a pastor's ministry qualification are based on areas of his personal life.

In most jobs, your personal life, morals, and what you do in your private time don't determine your employability. For a pastor, though, your personal character, home life, and private conduct qualify or disqualify you for your role. Scripture is clear in 1 Timothy 3:1–7 that a pastor must meet criteria such as being "above reproach, the husband of one wife, sober minded, self-controlled, respectable, hospitable" and "not a drunkard, not violent but gentle, not quarrelsome, not a lover of money" as well as family life that demonstrates he manages "his own household well" and even keeps "his children submissive." Titus 1:5–9 adds "not arrogant or quick-tempered" and "upright, holy, and disciplined."

---

6. Ibid.

A wrong decision in your personal life, problems in your marriage, or spiritual corruption in your heart can cause you to lose your job and hurt the testimony of Christ and the church in your community, especially if you crash out morally or ethically. So a healthy personal life is critical to a pastor's public ministry.

No one else is going to ensure that you maintain personal health.

You are a steward responsible to cultivate and protect your personal life so you can engage in long-term ministry. Most if not all of the areas of a pastor's personal health can only be cultivated and maintained by you. Others cannot or will not do it for you. Consider these examples.

Faithful and Fractured: Responding to the Clergy Health Crisis identifies four factors that enable pastors to flourish rather than burn out. They include focusing on big-picture mission, having a lot of social support (friends), paying close attention to your health, both physical and spiritual (including regular exercise, prayer, and devotions), and drawing clear boundaries around your personal, family, and rest times.[7]

Another resource, one I highly recommend, is *Resilient Ministry: What Pastors Told Us about Surviving and Thriving.* The authors spent seven years meeting with pastors discussing their personal lives, marriages, families and ministries. They identified five themes of surviving and thriving as a pastor: spiritual formation, self-care, emotional and cultural intelligence, marriage and family, and leadership and management.[8]

Looking over those two lists of contributing factors, I can identify several that only you can ensure are part of your life. Although other leaders and members of your church may generally desire your well-being, you are the one who has to take responsibility for these areas.

---

7. Rae Jean Proeschold-Bell and Jason Byassee, *Faithful and Fractured: Responding to the Clergy Health Crisis* (Baker Academic, 2018), 127–156. Proeschold-Bell is research director of the Duke Clergy Health Initiative. She and Byassee documented a decade of studies involving the health of pastors.

8. Bob Burns et al. *Resilient Ministry: What Pastors Told Us about Surviving and Thriving* (IVP, 2013), 19–25.

Churches need pastors.

The current dearth of available men to fill open pastoral positions is common knowledge. Combine that with the number of pastors leaving the ministry, and you have an ecclesiastical crisis. Additionally, many churches need revitalization, which requires a healthy pastor ready to engage in demanding ministry work. And there are many places where churches need to be planted. "The harvest is plentiful, but the laborers are few" (Matt 9:37). We need an increase in the number of men who are called, gifted, prepared, mature, and healthy to pastor these churches.

Healthy pastors generate healthy churches.

As is the pastor, so goes the church. If you are exhausted, stressed, sick, spiritually anemic, or have a strained marriage or family life, the church is going to reflect your lack of well-being. If your personal, family, and spiritual life are flourishing, even if your church is struggling, at least you will be in a better condition to address problems in a constructive and productive way.

Scriptural instructions, principles, and examples guide men in ministry to be proactive in cultivating their personal life for long-term ministry.

The Bible guides pastors toward stewarding their personal lives. In the next chapter we will look further into these scriptural truths.

Are you convinced? At least concerned? Will you join me as we look at the biblical basis, foundational principles, critical areas, and essential practices of being a healthy pastor?

REFLECT AND DISCUSS[9]

1. Is the idea of personal health something you have given much thought to? Discussed with others? Read about? Taken steps to improve?

2. Select two of the reasons for focusing on a pastor's personal health that stand out to you. Why are these significant?

3. Is there one specific area of pastoral health mentioned in this chapter that you know needs attention in your life? How do you hope this book will help you in that area?

---

9. I highly encourage you to use these prompts. Set aside time to think and pray through them. Additionally, great benefit can result from meeting with another pastor who is also reading through this book to discuss responses to these questions.

THE BIBLICAL BASIS AND DEFINITION OF A HEALTHY PASTOR

BIBLICAL BASIS

Did someone make up the idea of pastoral health so we can pamper ourselves, or is there a biblical basis for it? Consider two Bible texts that indicate it is a legitimate concern.[1]

3 John 1–2

The apostle John wrote the following to a church leader: "The elder to the beloved Gaius, whom I love in truth. Beloved, I pray that all may go well with you and that you may be in good health, as it goes well with your soul" (3 John 1–2).

Gaius was probably a leader in the church since John sent him a letter addressing church issues. John had prayed for this leader, specifically that "all may go well" with him. The Greek word εὐοδόω, translated "go well," literally means to "have a good journey." It denotes succeeding, moving forward, and making progress.

To "be in good health" refers to physical wellness. It's used in Scripture in contrast to being sick, such as in the case of the woman hemorrhaging

---

1. Subsequent chapters will address additional texts that emphasize personal health. These two texts are specifically relevant to church leaders.

blood (Mark 5:34) and the man with the withered hand (Matt 12:13). So "go well" is a general term for making good progress, and "good health" refers to being physically well. Then John added, "as it goes well with your soul." This phrase, "goes well," is the same as before when he prayed that "all may go well," but this time John used it to describe Gaius's soul—his ψυχή.

Note what Eduard Schweizer says regarding the use of ψυχή in 3 John 2: "We . . . have here a **distinction between the physical and the spiritual life** . . . ψυχή is the life which is ultimately important, i.e., which is **orientated to God**. Naturally ψυχή is not set in express antithesis to the bodily side here. The hope is that **the two will be in harmony**, not that they will be separated from one another."[2]

These comments distinguish the "soul" as our spiritual life, the life that is oriented toward God. "Just as it goes well with your soul" indicates that Gaius was thriving in his spiritual life—his relationship with God.

Now this greeting might sound like a generic opening to any written communication, such as starting an email with, "Hope you are well!" True, it was a normal salutation in ancient letters much like it is today. However, as D. Edmond Hiebert says, "Clearly John was not expressing a mere conventional health-wish but was giving personal utterance to a heart-felt prayer for Gaius."[3] These words of inspired Scripture represent the sincere heart of one Christian leader for the physical and spiritual health of another.

John prayed that Gaius would have general success, that he would be physically well, and that he would continue to have a thriving soul. Both spiritual and physical health are important enough for John to pray that his friend and church leader would be healthy and thrive in both. I think the content of John's prayer argues for church leaders, especially pastors, paying attention to their personal health, both spiritual and physical.

---

2. Eduard Schweizer, "ψυχή, ψυχικός, ἀνάψυξις, ἀναψύχω, δίψυχος, ὀλιγόψυχος," in *Theological Dictionary of the New Testament*, ed. Gerhard Kittel (Eerdmans, 1985), 9:651–52.

3. D. Edmond Hiebert, *The Epistles of John: An Expositional Commentary* (Bob Jones University Press, 1991), 323.

This is a good place to acknowledge that God in His providence has allowed some individuals to have disabilities, chronic physical ailments, or serious diseases. In these cases, their physical health is outside their control, and stewardship of their bodies will look different from others.

Matthew Henry provides helpful insight on this passage: "Grace and health are two rich companions; grace will improve health, health will employ grace. It frequently falls out that a rich soul is lodged in a crazy body." I think by *crazy* he meant unusual or abnormal. He is saying that often these physical challenges produce a depth of spiritual growth, "a rich soul."

He continues, "Grace must be exercised in submission to such a dispensation." By *dispensation* he is referring to the experience that has been sovereignly distributed to such people. God gives grace to those individuals to submit themselves to God's perfect plan for their lives. Many with life-altering disabilities and chronic diseases can give testimony to this grace and how God has used their experience to enrich their souls and give them opportunities to radiate that grace to others.

Henry concludes, "But we may well wish and pray that those who have prosperous souls may have healthful bodies too; their grace will shine in a larger sphere of activity."[4] In other words, being healthy in both body and soul will give you a broader, and I would add longer, ministry.

1 Timothy 4:12–16

Another text of Scripture highlights the fact that taking care of your personal life precedes and is essential to effective public ministry. In 1 Timothy 4:12–16, Paul urged Timothy to give focused attention to his personal condition before engaging in ministry to others.

> Let no one despise you for your youth, but set the believers an example in speech, in conduct, in love, in faith, in purity. Until I come, devote yourself to the public reading of Scripture, to exhortation, to teaching. Do not neglect the gift you have, which was

---

4. Matthew Henry, *Matthew Henry's Commentary on the Whole Bible: Complete and Unabridged in One Volume* (Hendrickson, 1991), 2458.

given you by prophecy when the council of elders laid their hands on you. Practice these things, immerse yourself in them, so that all may see your progress. Keep a close watch on yourself and on the teaching. Persist in this, for by so doing you will save both yourself and your hearers. (1 Timothy 4:12–16)

This visualization will help you see the two-fold emphasis on both personal life and public ministry.

PERSONAL	PUBLIC
Let no one despise you for your youth, but set the believers an example in speech, in conduct, in love, in faith, in purity	Until I come, devote yourself to the public reading of scripture, to exhortation, to teaching
Practice these things, immerse yourself in them	so that all may see your progress
Keep a close watch on yourself	and on the teaching
Persist in this, for by so doing you will save both yourself	and your hearers

As you can see, areas like speech, conduct, love, faith, and purity are all part of a pastor's personal life. "Keep a close watch on yourself" signifies our priority and responsibility to make sure our personal lives are in order.

DEFINITION OF PASTORAL HEALTH

Based on the above texts of Scripture, here's a definition we will build on through the rest of the book: Pastoral health is stewardship of your body and cultivation of your inner man in order to most effectively fulfill your calling to shepherd the flock of God.

In other words, a healthy pastor is physically well and has a thriving soul. You are responsible. You must steward your body and cultivate your inner man. Your personal health is up to you, and it is critical to effective pastoral ministry.

WHAT'S AHEAD?

In Part 2, Foundational Principles, we will talk about a pastor's source of identity, and then the concepts of self-care as stewardship and guarding your integrity. Part 3, Critical Areas identifies potential threats to a pastor's personal health, including a sense of unworthiness, ministry stress, discouragement, disappointment, comparison with others, and compassion fatigue. Part 4, Essential Practices encourages you to be proactive in communion with God, companionship in marriage, taking personal retreats, controlling your time, engaging in "holy distractions," disciplining yourself in physical habits, and cultivating holy companions. Part 5, Recovery and Final Prayer gives practical help essential to getting back what you've lost and concludes with my prayer for you.

REFLECT AND DISCUSS

1. Have you thought much before about the biblical emphasis on taking care of your body and personal life? What do you think about it based on this chapter?

2. Do you deal with any disabilities, chronic physical problems, or diseases? If so, how do you think these challenges can produce a "rich soul" in you as Matthew Henry describes?

3. What do you think of the definition of pastoral health in this chapter? Is it adequate? Is there anything you would change? Are you willing to pursue it?

PART 2

FOUNDATIONAL PRINCIPLES

CHAPTER THREE

A HEALTHY PASTOR'S SOURCE OF IDENTITY

THE CONCEPT OF IDENTITY

One of my hobbies is beekeeping. When my hives are thriving, I feel elation. A busy hive entrance with hundreds of foragers zipping off the landing board, beelining out toward fields of flowers, and returning laden with nectar and pollen; a queen filling the brood chamber with eggs that will soon produce tens of thousands of new workers; upper boxes heavy with sweet liquid gold—these make me feel like a good beekeeper. I walk away from a hive inspection with just a little swagger, toss my veil aside, and give my smoker a parting puff.

Then one day I find lifeless bee bodies on the ground outside the hive entrance. With concern I remove the cover. The bees seem anxious, subdued. As I check frames I find dead larvae in the cells. They look like little mummies. Chalkbrood![1] Eventually the colony dwindles down to a few hundred bees, and then they are gone. I have taken responsibility for these little creatures. It's my job to keep them healthy and strong. I have failed.

I feel good or bad depending on how my beehives are doing. My state of mind and sense of well-being are conditioned on the health of my bees.

---

1. Chalkbrood is a fungal disease that kills honey bee larvae. The mummy-like appearance of the dead larvae resembles tiny pieces of chalk. The state apiarist inspected my hives and said I had one of the worst cases of chalkbrood he had seen.

My identity as a beekeeper is closely connected to the condition of these little creatures.

One day a teaching colleague asked, "How are your bees doing?" I sadly told him of the demise of one of my hives. "I feel like a bad beekeeper," I said. His encouraging reply: "Thank the Lord that we don't have to get our identity from beehives!"

In a similar way, a pastor's identity is linked to his church. By identity, I am referring to his sense of who he is as a person.

Here's another example. Some teenagers like to cultivate an identity—who they view themselves to be, and who they want others to view them to be. A boy might like skateboarding. He not only invests in a certain brand of skateboard, he cultivates a look, including his clothes, shoes, hair, and attitude, and a group of like-minded friends. His life is wrapped up in skating.

Let's say his parents decide he is spending too much time on the board and not enough on schoolwork, and they're concerned about his friends' influence on him. They radically cut back his time at the skate park, make him tone down the look, and threaten to take away his wheels if he doesn't improve his grades. He erupts with anger, storms out of the room, and slams the door, yelling, "This is who I am!"

His identity is threatened. The loss of important aspects of boarding life diminishes his sense of individuality and worth. He has vested his value as a person in the persona of a skater.

REASONS PASTORS DERIVE IDENTITY FROM THEIR CHURCH

Let's relate this idea of identity to being a pastor. Generally men find a sense of individuality and worth in their work. This can be uniquely true of a pastor for several reasons. **One reason is the close association of his role as a pastor with his relationship with God.** Ministry is a calling, not a chosen profession. A man goes into ministry in response to God's work in his life. The daily responsibilities of ministry require dependence on God. A pastor cultivates a stronger than average prayer life. He studies the Scriptures almost every day preparing sermons and seeking wisdom essential to shepherding his people and leading the church. He may view the church as an extension of his relationship with God.

When the church is thriving, or at least running smoothly, it seems God is blessing the pastor's faithfulness, answering his prayers, and rewarding his labor with a fruitful harvest. But conflicts, member loss, criticism, financial shortfalls, and an unused baptistry feel like failure. These indicators seem to signal the loss of God's blessing and to reflect that the pastor's relationship with God is less than optimal.

Another reason a pastor's sense of identity is affected by his church is the inconsistent nature of people. Think about it this way. Let's say a pastor determines to equip the saints for the work of ministry in order to build up the body of Christ, cultivate unity in the church, and develop his church toward resembling Christ corporately in order to represent Him in the community. This pursuit reflects Paul's description of a pastor's role in Ephesians 4:11–13. The pastor can be committed, disciplined, prayerful, diligent, passionate, and strategic in pursuing this objective, but success depends on other people.

In fact, I see several links in this chain of objectives that rely on church members' willingness and involvement.

- There must be saints to equip—people who have heard and believed the gospel and placed themselves under the shepherding care of the church.

- These people must be receptive and responsive to the equipping work of the pastor—his preaching, teaching, and leadership.

- They must be committed to investing time and energy into the work of ministry, actual labor, that contributes to the life and health of the church.

- They must not have a self-centered attitude but be concerned for the church's health and growth. They must not have a divisive influence but work at unity.

- They must be maturing individually in order to help the church mature corporately.

Ideally every member of the church would be 100 percent engaged in these pursuits. But we know the reality. There is a gap between the pastor's goals for his church and people's interest in pursuing them. Some people even resist the pastor's leadership in guiding the church to pursue these goals. If a pastor is fulfilling his leadership role the best he can, but the church is not making progress toward ministry, unity, and maturity, then he might draw the conclusion he is not a good pastor. He considers himself to be the reason the church is struggling and may even question his fitness for ministry.

REMEDIES FOR DERIVING YOUR IDENTITY FROM YOUR CHURCH

Let's think about how to remedy the mindset in which a pastor derives his identity from the condition of his church. What is your true identity?

First, you are a man.

You are a created being with all the limitations associated with your finite nature. You can't know everything, be everywhere, or fix everyone. You have not completely vanquished sin's influence in your own heart, and you cannot eradicate the effects of sin from the lives of others.

What you can do is cultivate growth in your inner man, proactively engage in submission to God in your life, and encourage others to do the same, recognizing people will make their own choices and experience the corresponding blessings or consequences.

Second, you are a man in Christ.

The profound doctrine of your union with Christ establishes your true identity. Before you were installed as the pastor of your church, you became what Paul called himself, "a man in Christ" (2 Cor 12:2). You were dead in your sins, but you have been made alive together with Christ (Eph 2:1–7). You have been joined in the death of Christ, raised into life with Him, and now walk in newness of life (Rom 6:1–5).

I want to encourage you to elevate the truth of your union with Christ in your mind. Romans 6:11 says, "Consider yourselves dead to sin and alive to God in Christ Jesus." In other words, engage in a mental calculation, and keep reminding yourself of your union with Christ and its effects.

You naturally think about your attachment to your church and its effect on you, especially during hard seasons. When church is up, you're up, and when it's down, you're down. But who you are, including your emotions, your state of mind, and your sense of well-being is not linked to the ups and downs of your church. It is not tied to whether a counselee is responding to your exhortations. It does not depend on the comments, or lack thereof, in response to your last sermon.

Let me relate this to an experience I had with my preaching ministry. I recently served as an interim pastor in a struggling church for a little over a year. My role was not only to fill a gap between pastors, but to help the church grow and be able to call a pastor. Progress was very slow. I did not know if my efforts were yielding any fruit at all.

There were times when my wife and I each said to the other on the way to church on Sunday mornings, "I don't know if I can keep doing this." I often felt like I was preaching into the air. One Sunday when I was wrestling with these doubts, I thought, *I'm going to preach for the Lord. It doesn't matter if anyone is listening, or if what I say results in any change. This sermon is for God. He is my audience. I will preach my heart out for Him.*

That's what I did, and numerous times afterward. Our ministry there finished, and I still don't know what real impact we had. But I was helped by the realization that I can pour out my life, exercise my gifts, and labor hard regardless of whether anyone notices or cares. The satisfaction that I derive from preaching can come from the act of presenting it to the Lord as my service to Him rather than from my perception of how others view it or are impacted by it. My identity is in my relationship with Christ, not what others think of me.

The same is true of any part of your ministry. Of course we want to have an impact. It's encouraging when we see fruit. But ultimately we minister in the grace of Christ and for the glory of Christ.

Third, you are a member of the body of Christ.

Pastor, you are a man, and you are a man in Christ. Here is what 1 Corinthians 12:13 says about you: "For in one Spirit we were all baptized into one body—Jews or Greeks, slaves or free—and all were made to drink of one Spirit." Paul emphasized that all kinds and categories of people are united together into the body of Christ, which is the church. I think it's appropriate to paraphrase what he wrote by adding "lay people and pastors." You, pastor, have been baptized by the Holy Spirit into the body of Christ along with every other member. You are not separate from the church.

You belong to the "one new man" which is the body of Christ, the church, that Paul described in Ephesians 2:11–14. Listen to what he said about you: "But now in Christ Jesus you who once were far off have been brought near by the blood of Christ. For he himself is our peace, who has made us both one and has broken down in his flesh the dividing wall of hostility." Any distance between you and God and any hostility between you and others has been abolished by the cross!

You are not just part of the church because you work there. Your primary relationship with the church is not as an employee or an organizational leader or a spokesperson. Pastors can feel isolated from church life because of their up-front activity and their overseeing role. Church people may forget their pastor is a church member just like they are. He should enjoy the benefits and blessings of church life right along with them.

Our tendency as pastors is to view church through managerial eyes. We look at everything critically, noticing the weeds in the landscaping, the clock that hasn't been changed with Daylight Savings Time, the late-running music practice, the technology glitches during the service, and the not-so-friendly way visitors are treated. We feel the tension of these as if the church were an extension of ourselves. Anything that goes wrong is a personal reflection on us.

Let me encourage you to make some mental adjustments regarding how you view church life. Make a conscious choice to enter into the life of the body of Christ as a member, not just as a leader. Here are some ways to adjust your thinking about church.

CONSIDER CONGREGATIONAL SINGING

You may be involved in planning and even leading the musical worship in your church. Find a way to engage your heart, mind, and voice in true worship when it is time to sing. Of course this is easiest if someone else is leading. You are blessed if your church has a person who can do this.

One of my favorite changes in church cultures I've been part of during the past couple of decades is the shift to pastors sitting with the congregation except when they are speaking to the group. I used to sit on the platform, elevated above everyone else, facing the crowd. When visiting another church on a Sunday, I observed the lead pastor sitting on the front row of the regular seats. I thought, *I want to do that.* So when we moved into a new space, I started a new tradition and sat with my church instead of conspicuously in front of everyone. Facing the same direction, lifting my voice right alongside theirs, positioned me to engage my own mind and heart in exalting God together with them rather than feeling I was on display. Worshiping next to my wife is an extra blessing.

Try to turn off manager mode while you sing, in which you are alert to all the little things that go wrong or could be done better. Sure, if there's a problem that needs to be addressed, maybe jot it down on your order of service to follow up on later. Then forget it and go back to worshiping Jesus.

Let the lyrics with their profound meaning captivate your thoughts and swell your heart. Lift your voice, and let it rip! Enjoy praising God and pour out your soul in adoration and thanks. Stop thinking about how you're going to introduce your sermon in a few minutes and worship your Savior and Lord.

INTAKE OF THE PREACHING AND TEACHING OF THE WORD

Another area in which to function as a member of the body of Christ is by your intake of the preaching and teaching of the Word. If you're a lead pastor, you likely preach the Word nearly every Sunday. The public ministry of the Word is a major part of your shepherding work. You can of course listen to recorded preaching on your own during the week. But there's something healthy about sitting with a congregation or class while someone else opens the Word and feeds your soul as a member of the body of Christ. Situations vary, and options may be limited. You might be the only member of your church with the maturity and skill to teach the Scriptures. But if your church is blessed with others who can teach or preach, it is a healthy practice to periodically place yourself under their ministry.

Why would you do this? Because you are a growing Christian who needs to be fed. Because you are a church member who benefits from the gifts of others. Because you need a break.

Preaching the Word is one of the most exhilarating and at the same time one of the most draining aspects of your work as a pastor. You are pouring out your whole being when you preach. Every Christian needs to be spiritually nourished with the Word through gifted members of the body. Pastors especially need their spiritual strength replenished.

Schedule assistant pastors to speak, not only when you're on a trip. Take a quarter and sit in a Sunday school class or Bible study you aren't leading. A pastor should overcome feelings of guilt or laziness that might pop up when he's not preaching. Listening to the Word with the body of Christ is healthy.

COMMUNITY

Another way to exercise your identity as a member of the body of Christ is through community, also known as fellowship. When our church started small groups that met in homes on a weeknight to discuss Sunday's sermon and pray for each other, my wife and I determined that we would belong to one without being the ones to lead it. Now we would have if needed, but thankfully there were enough leaders that we could just participate. This freed us to converse, discuss, pray, and enjoy the company of others without the pressure of making things happen.

I think it helps a pastor's well-being to engage in community when it isn't his job. Even lobby conversations after church can feel like work for a pastor. Sometimes imagine you aren't on the clock on a Sunday morning after church. Sure, stand at the door and shake hands for a while. Then plop down in that chair grouping with whoever is there and just talk. Enjoy knowing other Christians for who they are and sharing yourself with others as a fellow believer.

COMMUNION

Communion is a powerful reminder of your identity as a member of the body of Christ. If you're like me, leading the Lord's Supper brings a great sense of privilege and joy. If it has become a perfunctory ritual, clear time in your schedule to meditate prayerfully on the price Jesus paid for *you* and the benefits His sacrifice provides to *you*. Personalize it before publicly presiding over it.

Then while leading your people through the significance of the elements and prompting them to follow the instructions Christ gave for partaking, keep in mind the togetherness of observing communion. "Take and eat" together and "Let's all drink" together unify *you* with your brothers and sisters in the Lord.

I presented a workshop session on this topic to a group of pastors. One of them said he purposely has a deacon periodically lead communion so he can enjoy the blessing of participating without the pressure of leading it. Good idea!

FINANCIAL GIVING

You can also practice your identity as a member of the body through the act of financial giving. Far from merely an obligation, our contributions are a vital part of church life. Even though pastors are paid by the church, we can experience the joy of giving just as much as every other member. That money becomes ours to do with whatever we choose. We can squander it, save it, spend it, or share it. Our voluntary choice to support gospel work and help others in need brings joy to God, helps His work move forward, and encourages the hearts of those who serve and those who lack. Every dollar makes a difference, and your contribution combines with all the others as an offering to God and an investment producing inestimable eternal dividends.

SERVING

One more way I'll suggest to function consciously as a member in the body of Christ while pastoring is by serving. Church members serve in the body, applying their gifts and dedicating their time and energy to build up the body of Christ and accomplish the work of ministry. A pastor can fall into viewing ministry work as his job. True, pastoring is a vocation and may be considered a profession. The fact that our daily work is for the church tends to diminish the mentality of serving. After all, we are salaried employees, not volunteers.

Let's keep in mind that regardless of role, every member ultimately serves the Lord Jesus Christ. Additionally, we all do our part to help the church grow. And we are serving others, not just an organization or a cause. "Be fervent in spirit, serve the Lord" (Rom 12:11) is an exhortation for all members, including pastors, to bear in mind. Pastor, what is your identity? You are a man. You are a man in Christ. You are a member of the body of Christ.

Fourth, you are a person who lives in this world with normal human roles to fill.

Depending on your individual circumstances, these may include husband, father, neighbor, and community member. Take away your church, and this is still you. If you get fired, or your church closes, the relationships you have with the people closest to you can remain intact.

So at the end of the day, go home, and be that man. When you back out of the garage for an evening visit, counseling appointment, or deacon meeting, look forward to falling into bed later next to the woman you love with all your heart, who will be beside you come hell or high water. Blow a Saturday goofing off with your kids. Hang out in your neighbor's back yard over a cold ginger ale. Indulge in the things God has given you "richly . . . to enjoy" (1 Tim 6:17).

Linking your identity—who you see yourself to be as a person and as a Christian—to the church is dangerous for a pastor. It will erode your confidence in your relationship with God and your ability to persevere in ministry. Remind yourself often that "your life is hidden with Christ in God" (Col 3:3). Balance the stress of ministry work with the blessing of knowing you are a member of Christ's body, of which He is the head. Enjoy life as the man God made you to be.

REFLECT AND DISCUSS

1. What stands out to you from the reasons pastors derive their identity from their church? Why?

2. How does the truth of your union with Christ help you think about ministry?

3. Are there one or two practical ways to live out your membership in the body of Christ that are helpful to you? Which ones and why?

CHAPTER FOUR

SELF-CARE AS STEWARDSHIP

"Self-care," a popular term that relates to personal health, sounds like man-centered psychobabble. It feels inherently selfish and seems to contradict the biblical concepts of self-denial and self-sacrifice. Why would a ministry-minded Christian pay special attention to himself?

Before we reject it, let's learn what self-care is, then see if any part of it aligns with Scripture. Perhaps it belongs on the trash pile of worldly philosophies. Or possibly common grace has made mankind instinctively conscious of a healthy practice that pastors should consider. By the end of this chapter I hope you will see that appropriate self-care is essential to stewardship of your personal life for longevity in ministry.

UNDERSTANDING SELF-CARE

A helpful definition of self-care is "the self-initiated behavior that people choose to incorporate to promote good health and general well-being."[1] Simply stated, self-care is taking responsibility for your own health and well-being and actively pursuing, maintaining, and protecting it.

Three areas are usually in focus. These are physical well-being, including diet, exercise, and sleep; mental and psychological well-being, especially how one deals with stress; and relational well-being, harmony and satis-

---

1. Jason Mills, Timothy Ward, and Jennifer N. Fraser, "Exploring the Meaning and Practice of Self-Care Among Palliative Care Nurses and Doctors: a Qualitative Study," https://www.ncbi.nlm.nih.gov/pmc/articles/PMC5907186/.

faction in relationships with family, friends, and others. As Christians, we add a fourth, spiritual well-being, which includes communion with God and spiritual formation.

QUESTIONS ABOUT SELF-CARE

Two questions arise when relating self-care to pastors. Does pastoral life increase the need for self-care? And is self-care a legitimate pursuit for a Christian in ministry?

As we consider the first question, we'll focus on the "self" element of self-care in a way that distinguishes it from self-centeredness. "Self" denotes the care of one's self, but it also emphasizes that the individual is proactive in performing this care. That's the part I want to focus on—the individual's initiative. One practicing self-care doesn't wait for a medical professional, family member, or other outside entity to look after his physical or mental well-being.

In the case of a pastor engaging in self-care, he doesn't rely on other church leaders or his doctor to tell him he needs to cut back on seventy-hour workweeks, eat more whole foods, and go for a bike ride with his family. He takes charge of his priorities and schedule and orders his life to fulfill his pastoral role while maintaining balanced personal health.

Herein lies the problem for pastors. The very nature of their vocation is to serve others. They pour out their time and energy every day for church members and anyone else who seems to need assistance. One text message can disrupt his day or even an entire week depending on the degree of calamity it conveys. Stress levels fluctuate drastically, sometimes from one minute to the next.

You can probably identify with these stress-inducing factors that fill a pastor's schedule:

> Twelve hour workdays; supervisory relationships requiring managerial and delegation skills; unpredictable schedule; people seeking help with serious problems; inability to take extended breaks from ministry work, or guilt feelings when you do; numerous

meetings; expectation of availability to church members; enlisting and overseeing volunteers; being a good leader; addressing and resolving conflicts; performing work without appropriate skill set; working with political forces in the church; taking criticism; performing sacred work;[2] poor diet; poor exercise habits; career uncertainty; role ambiguity; role conflict (between church expectations and personal or family needs); role overload (too many real or imagined expectations); lack of opportunities to 'derole' and be yourself for a change; loneliness; time management frustrations; life-change stressors; temptations of all kinds (sexual, despair if your church isn't growing, jealousy of the success of others, anxiety over financial problems, anger, to name a few).[3]

And, of course, Sunday's coming!

The authors of *Resilient Ministry* conclude, "If we combine the expectations of this role with the fact that most pastors are people-pleasers, we can understand how ministry can feel like a never-ending treadmill of trying to satisfy others whose expectations cannot be met."[4]

During the COVID pandemic of 2020, pastoral stress levels shot up. Anxiety, depression, and resignation from ministry altogether increased as a result of dealing with COVID-related issues in the church.

Even before COVID, according to a Barna Group report *The State of Pastors*, published in 2017, one out of three pastors were at risk of burnout and almost one half faced depression.[5]

Pastors are especially susceptible to work and lifestyle patterns that wear them down physically, mentally, emotionally, and spiritually. And, though many church members are affectionate toward their pastors, they are not

---

2. Proeschold-Bell and Byassee, 1–16.

3. "Stress and Burnout in Ministry," http://www.jmm.org.au/articles/8200. htm.

4. Burns et al., 62.

5. Barna Group, *The State of Pastors: How Today's Faith Leaders are Navigating Life and Leadership in an Age of Complexity* (Barna, 2017), 11.

likely to realize that daily ministry life is a threat to pastors' health and well-being. It would be a very unusual setting in which the chairman of the deacons asked the pastor for a report of his schedule and then said, "You need to get seven hours of sleep a night and spend more time with your family. We need to hire an assistant pastor. And by the way, this summer we're sending you on a six-week rest and study sabbatical."

A typical congregation isn't aware their pastor is redlining until he's in the ER with chest pains, or he abruptly resigns on a Sunday morning. The reality is pastors must take responsibility for gauging their health indicators and maintaining their own routines to preserve and protect their well-being.

Does pastoral life increase the need for self-care? I think the answer to that is pretty clear. Pastors are high risk candidates for burning out or just wearing out and bailing out. Even with a caring congregation and supportive leadership team, every pastor needs to take responsibility for his own personal health and take the initiative to maintain it.

What about the second question? Is self-care a legitimate pursuit for a Christian in ministry?

We're good with terms like self-denial, self-discipline, and self-control. These are biblically-based concepts. But self-care? It sounds like you're taking yourself to a spa. Announce at the end of a Sunday service, and you'll get a reaction for sure: "I'm taking a few days off this week for self-care." Right.

The common mentality about Christian living, and especially vocational ministry, is anything that caters to self is bad. Self is the enemy, second only to the Devil. Anything that appeals to self is automatically suspect. Self-indulgent practices are guilty pleasures. Soldiers of the cross endure hardship, and they'd better not be caught reading fiction or taking a nap.

How could self-care be legitimate for one called to the rigors of ministry? This is where a secular term can blur our perspective of a valid idea. Self-care sounds like you're being soft on yourself, avoiding difficulty, and putting your own needs first. Of course, all of these are the opposite of biblical principles, especially love, which is giving yourself, not coddling yourself.

Let's answer the question of self-care as a legitimate pursuit by considering a concept that is rooted in Scripture.

A BIBLICALLY-BASED PERSPECTIVE OF SELF-CARE

Does self-care have any place in a pastor's life? If viewed solely from a human perspective, maybe in a very limited way. But viewed through a biblical lens, self-care is very like the concept of stewardship.

Self-care, viewed biblically, is stewardship of your personal resources and priorities. It is managing the resources God has entrusted to you for eternal benefit. Several Bible texts come to mind.

> The parable of the talents teaches us to invest the resources entrusted to us for the benefit of the Master. If we steward our abilities, time, and opportunities well, we are rewarded with our Lord's words, "Well done, good and faithful servant. You have been faithful over a little; I will set you over much. Enter into the joy of your master" (Matt 25:21).

> Peter exhorts us to use our gifts not only in a way that benefits others, but as good stewards of what God has graciously entrusted to us. "As each one has received a special gift, employ it in serving one another as good stewards of the manifold grace of God" (1 Pet 4:10 NASB).

> Paul taught that our physical bodies are a means of glorifying God. "Your body is a temple of the Holy Spirit . . . you are not your own. For you have been bought with a price: therefore glorify God in your body" (1 Cor 6:19–20 NASB).

> Jethro guided Moses to alter his leadership style radically or he would burn out and hurt the people he was supposed to be helping. "What is this that you are doing for the people? Why do you sit alone, and all the people stand around you from morning till evening? . . . What you are doing is not good. You and the peo-

ple with you will certainly wear yourselves out, for the thing is too heavy for you. You are not able to do it alone" (Exod 18:14, 17–18).

Jesus instructed His disciples to "'Come aside by yourselves to a deserted place and rest a while.' For there were many coming and going, and they did not even have time to eat" (Mark 6:31 NKJV).

Paul mentored Timothy to pay careful attention to his personal life so he would have an effective public ministry. "Pay close attention to yourself and to your teaching" (1 Tim 4:16 NASB). He also instructed Timothy to treat physical health issues and prevent them if possible. "No longer drink only water, but use a little wine for your stomach's sake and your frequent infirmities" (1 Tim 5:23 NKJV).

These instructions and examples provide a pattern for considering stewardship of our physical as well as spiritual resources in order to glorify God and persevere in ministry.

Here is a helpful definition of pastoral self-care that reflects a biblical perspective: "The wisdom to ensure, as far as humanly possible, a wise and orderly work that conserves and lengthens a pastor's ministry."[6] One can view this stewardship as "the ongoing development of the whole person, including the emotional, spiritual, relational, physical, and intellectual areas of life."[7] Another author describes it as "attending to and respecting the limitations and needs that God has designed for humans . . . simply caring for God's crowning creation, the human machine."[8]

The secular concept of self-care is the world's recognition of what Christians already know. God endowed His creatures with sufficient yet limited

---

6. Peter Brain, *Going the Distance: How to Stay Fit For a Lifetime of Ministry* (GoodBook Company, 2001), 24.

7. Burns et al., 61.

8. Nathan Foster, "Selfish Care, Self-Care, and Soul Care—What's the Difference?" https://renovare.org/articles/selfish-care-vs-soul-care.

capacity to serve and glorify Him. We are responsible to manage our lives in a way that sustains a lifetime of effective ministry.

Stewardship is taking responsibility for maintaining areas of your personal life so you will burn on rather than burn out.[9] You manage your life for long-term ministry. You see the need for it, you take the initiative, you make choices, and you live accordingly.

The idea of self-care can be helpful, but it needs to be seen as a form of stewardship, and it requires a God-focused rather than a self-centered perspective. This chart demonstrates the distinction between self-care and stewardship.

SELF-CARE	STEWARDSHIP
Take care of yourself.	Take care of yourself for long-term service to God.
Eat, sleep, and exercise to maintain physical health.	Take care of your physical body with nutrition, rest, and exercise because it is the temple of God for the purpose of long-term ministry.
Set boundaries to protect your personal life. (Boundaries are a significant element of secular self-care.)	Set boundaries to ensure you invest appropriate time in all priorities, relationships, and responsibilities for the glory of God.

BALANCING SERVANTHOOD WITH STEWARDSHIP

An idea that is often associated with ministry is servant leadership. This is a biblical concept, but it must be kept in balance.

The concept of servant leadership, if misapplied, can threaten a pastor's stewardship of his personal life. Some may have the idea that because we

---

9. Burns et al., 61.

are supposed to be servants, as Jesus taught in Mark 10:42–45, we should be available to anyone at any time. Other people's needs or expectations take precedence. This concept has been instilled in many of us, possibly resulting in a diminished view of stewardship. Herein lies a tension in a pastor's life—balancing servanthood and stewardship.

According to a servant mindset, pastors feel they should always be available to respond to needs. However, pastors need to understand and practice stewardship as well, proactively choosing how to manage their resources—time, energy, and abilities—to honor God, serve others, and sustain long-term ministry.

Consider the following comparison that demonstrates the tension between servanthood and stewardship:

SERVANTHOOD	STEWARDSHIP
Horizontal (others) and vertical (God)	Vertical (God)
Need-focused—what is desired or expected of me and how I should fulfill it	Resources-focused—what has been entrusted to me and how I should use it
Put others first, before yourself—I am available to others	Put God first, above all—I am accountable to God first
Responds to needs	Takes responsibility—often but not always responding to others' needs
Gives	Manages, invests—How should I invest my time, gifts, energy?
Immediate	Long-term, eternal

Motivated to please people	Motivated by giving account to God
My time is yours—"open door" policy	My time is God's
May be motivated by pressure, guilt	Motivated by wisdom—making wise choices, not based on guilt
What others see	What God knows—not controlled by expectations, real or perceived
Almost always says yes; hardly ever says no	Often says yes; sometimes graciously says no
Lets others set agenda	Sets an agenda that includes others

Both servanthood and stewardship are taught in Scripture, so they are both valid approaches to life and ministry. It seems to me servanthood fits within stewardship. Culturally the steward, or household manager, was one of the servants. So a steward was in the position of a servant. He carried out his responsibilities as a servant by being a good steward. Servants can be wise stewards, and stewards can be faithful servants.

PRACTICAL STEWARDSHIP

On the practical side, what does stewarding your personal resources for long-term ministry look like? Here's a checklist.

- Sufficient rest
- Healthful diet
- Regular exercise

- Consistent and meaningful personal devotions

- Spiritual growth

- Appropriate commitments of time, energy, and attention to marriage, family, ministry, and friendships, along with discernment in saying yes or no when necessary[10]

Rather than allowing others' needs and expectations to determine a pastor's schedule, he establishes a reasonable plan including time for personal devotion, family, exercise, and a date with his wife as well as sermon preparation, discipleship meetings, and hospital and homebound visits. A true emergency may alter his plans, but he works the usual requests for his time around the priorities he has established.

Is self-care a legitimate pursuit for a Christian in ministry? If the self-care we're talking about is not self-indulgence, but stewardship, then yes. A pastor should maintain his physical body, inner man, and personal life for long-term ministry for the glory of God.

---

10. We will address these in subsequent chapters.

CHAPTER FOUR

REFLECT AND DISCUSS

1. What do you think about the concept of stewardship related to your personal life? How would you describe your stewardship of your health? Are there ways you would like to become a better steward?

2. This chapter states, "The secular concept of self-care is the world's recognition of what Christians already know. God endowed His creatures with sufficient yet limited capacity to serve and glorify Him. We are responsible to manage our lives in a way that sustains a lifetime of effective ministry." Do you agree or disagree? Why?

3. Select two to three areas from the table comparing servanthood and stewardship that you would like to give serious consideration to. Pray for wisdom in how you might balance being a servant with being a steward in these areas.

CHAPTER FIVE

GUARDING INTEGRITY FOR A PERSEVERING MINISTRY

Crash and burn. Another one bites the dust. "Did you hear about . . .?" Accusations of financial impropriety, sexual misconduct, or verbal abuse erupt. Another pastor flames out and tumbles into oblivion.

The public demise of pastors should provoke us to examine our hearts and subject our own lives to scrutiny. Whether a nationally-acclaimed figure or just your average pastor, his fall has a negative impact on the name of Christ and His church.

Thousands of pastors quit. Scores of men in ministry fail. How can you and I persevere? What measures can we take to not only avoid a crash, but cross the finish line with our integrity and ministry intact?

WATCH YOURSELF

The importance of personal integrity for pastors is nothing new. Paul looked the very first pastors in the church of Ephesus in the eye and said, "Watch yourselves." The complete instruction goes like this: "Therefore take heed to yourselves and to all the flock, among which the Holy Spirit has made you overseers, to shepherd the church of God which He purchased with His own blood" (Acts 20:28, NKJV).

The admonition "take heed" means to be alert and on guard, like Secret Service agents assigned to protect the POTUS when he exits his limo. They are alert to potential danger and ready to do anything necessary to protect him. In a similar way, pastors must be alert and on guard against threats to their integrity as well as their ministry.

"Yourselves" in Paul's instruction identifies the pastors' personal lives. They were to watch over themselves "and . . . all the flock," but their personal lives were the first priority. Just as there were threats to the church—"fierce wolves will come in among you, not sparing the flock" (v. 29)—there were also enemies who would take out a pastor. That hasn't changed. Pastor, you are a target. You are prey. Watch yourself.

Paul messaged Timothy the same challenge with more details.

> Let no one despise you for your youth, but set the believers an example in speech, in conduct, in love, in faith, in purity. . . . Keep a close watch on yourself and on the teaching. Persist in this, for by so doing you will save both yourself and your hearers. (1 Tim 4:12, 16)

There it is again: "Watch yourself." Paul addressed both Timothy's personal life and public ministry. The order is important. "Yourself . . . and the teaching." To the Ephesian pastors, it was "Take heed to yourselves and to all the flock of God." Watch your personal life, then take care of the church. Church responsibilities and problems can weigh a pastor down, but if his personal life is strong, he will be much less likely to fall. He will be able to persevere.

In his exhortation to Timothy, Paul pointed out specific areas every pastor, whether young or old, should pay attention to. His flow of thought starts in verse 12. Notice several areas of a pastor's personal life that require careful attention to maintain integrity and persevere in ministry.

Watch Out for Immaturity

"Let no one despise you for your youth" means don't give anyone a reason to disregard your message because of your age. In the early years of a man's ministry, he is prone to make impulsive decisions, implement abrupt changes, make offensive comments (even unintentionally), and be insensitive to people's feelings. It takes time to establish a record of solid teaching, respectable character, and sound decisions. People are often slow to trust a young man in ministry. He will also be vulnerable to temptations common to early manhood which can lead to moral failure.

Pastor, watch yourself, especially in early adulthood and the first years of ministry. Earn credibility. Cultivate trust. Build respect. One way to do this is to serve as an assistant for several years before becoming a lead pastor. A few young men can successfully go straight from college or seminary into a lead pastor position. But most need several years to mature personally and learn ministry.

The number of young pastors who leave ministry is saddening. Possibly they expect too much of themselves and break under the pressure of pastoral ministry without personal maturity. A new graduate who starts out as an assistant chooses wisely. Churches can help young men mature by creating positions and providing financially for them to serve while growing in maturity. Pastors who start well will be more likely to persevere.

Watch Your Outward Life

The challenge to Timothy and to all pastors includes, "Set the believers an example" (1 Tim 4:12). Pastors impact people not only by their public ministry but also by their day-to-day actions.

"In speech" probably refers to their personal communication. Pastors are known for their preaching. Their conversations should also be gracious and edifying. It is sad to hear of prominent pastors who, to close associates or in unscripted moments, are known for explosive anger, profanity, insults, and intimidation.

Pastors should model how growing believers live. This includes in their speech. Anyone under the sound of a pastor's public ministry should also be able to observe him in private conversation using speech that is "always . . . gracious" (Col 4:6).

Guard your mouth. Don't speak in haste. Even when other people's words sting you, don't respond in kind. Speak truth but make sure it is "in love" (Eph 4:15). In tense situations, choose words that are "patient and kind," not envious, not boastful, "not arrogant or rude," not insisting on your "own way," "not irritable or resentful," not rejoicing "at wrongdoing," but rejoicing in the truth (1 Cor 13:4–6).

"Conduct" is what people around you observe. A pastor's behavior should enhance his message, not contradict it. A pastor whose ministry is either thriving or suffering might justify fleshly indulgences. These can erode credibility and lead to disaster.

A megachurch near where I used to pastor drew people by the thousands to its multiple campuses. The hip pastor used hologram technology to preach to all services at once. His ministry became nationally known for innovative methodology and numerical success. Edgy sermon topics, coarse language, and permissive lifestyle choices generated a bad boy pastor persona. After sixteen years at the church he started, this pastor made headlines when he was fired for alcohol abuse. Instances like this are a strong reminder to "watch yourselves."

Watch Your Inner Life

The essence of "love" (1 Tim 4:12) is unselfishness. It shows up as consideration for others, generosity, and willingness to sacrifice personal comfort in order to provide what others need. Looking out for others is expected of a pastor. It goes with the job. If we are not careful, we can put on a loving act while allowing selfishness to grow in our hearts. A backstory often surfaces in the wake of a pastoral crash that reveals a series of self-centered choices. Pastoral longevity is the result of a lifetime of putting others ahead of self.

"Faith" is personal trust in God not only for salvation, but for daily life and growth as a believer. The basic practices of a life of faith are essential to a pastor's spiritual well-being. These include worshiping God, communing with God through meditation on His Word and prayer, and living in community with other believers.

Pastors are often up front leading during church gatherings. They spend many hours a week in sermon preparation. They're busy overseeing the community aspects of the church's life. Participating personally in the essentials of a life of faith can be challenging for a pastor. Consider these approaches to keeping your personal walk with God fresh:[1]

- Spend significant time on your day off reading and meditating on Scripture without the pressure of sermon preparation.

- Take a walk outdoors a few times a week and have a conversation with God. Talk to Him like you would a friend. Open your heart and express your burdens, questions, and joys.

- Involve others in leading church services so you can sit with the congregation and engage your own heart in worship before you get up to preach.

- Attend a conference or two a year where your own soul can be fed by good preaching.

- Cultivate a few close friendships in which you are encouraged spiritually.

"Faith" in 1 Timothy 4:12 also includes a pastor's trust in God and His Word rather than in his own talents, personality, or strategic plans. Pastors often reach the end of themselves. The demanding schedule, stressful counseling issues, labor of sermon preparation, and other rigors of shepherding work have an exhausting effect. Even if you don't burn out, you might just wear out.

Pastors who persevere learn to trust God. You are one man. Let Jesus build His church. Your church's growth and success depend on Him.

You preach to your people that they should have faith in God during trials. Pastor, your church's demands and difficulties are your trial. Adopt

---

1. These are addressed more completely in other chapters, but they bear repeating!

the attitude of Paul when he said, "We were so utterly burdened beyond our strength that we despaired of life itself. Indeed we felt that we had received the sentence of death. But that was to make us rely not on ourselves but on God who raised the dead" (2 Cor 1:8–9). Work hard, but trust God.

When you find yourself growing weak, starting to indulge in thoughts or choices that you know will lead to disaster, turn to your Father in faith. Openly acknowledge your need for help. Call on Him for grace in your time of need. He is the faithful one. You can trust Him to forgive you, renew your strength, and enable you to press on.

Watch Your Moral Purity

"Purity" in 1 Timothy 4:12 probably means moral purity. Paul used the same word a few verses later in chapter 5, verse 2, warning Timothy to treat the "younger women as sisters, in all purity." A pastor's watch over himself includes keeping himself relationally and sexually pure.

Here's the all too familiar scenario: a pastor's imagination is ensnared by sensual images on social media or in movie scenes. Down the path of impurity he goes from guilty glimpses to hours of pornographic fantasy. His conscience burns. Spiritual vitality drains away. As impurity poisons his soul, his relationships turn cold and ministry work becomes meaningless. A crash is imminent.

Guarding against a fall in this area starts in your heart. "Love," which is seeking the good of others rather than yourself, and "faith," which is trust in God and daily personal growth (both in verse 13 of chapter 4) enable you to practice "purity."[2]

One of the best practical ways to guard your viewing is to have accountability software on phones, tablets, and computers. Enlist a partner who sees a report of every site you visit. Software won't stop a determined pornography viewer, but it provides a safeguard for the man who is endeavoring to stay pure.

---

2. See chapter 12 on "Communion with God" for more on developing your love for God as a guard against sin.

Purity includes guarding the "husband of one wife" qualification for pastors (1 Tim 3:2). The term literally means "one-woman man." A persevering pastor cultivates and protects exclusive devotion to his spouse. Companionship and intimacy are often casualties in a ministry marriage. Unless both husband and wife work at these, their hearts may become vulnerable to inappropriate friendships, emotional affairs, and adultery. Sadly, this kind of ministry crash has become so common it's hardly a shock anymore.

Determine together that you will prioritize your marriage. Plan and take time to be together on dates, outings, and getaways. Pray together. Listen to one another. Have fun. Guard yourself, pastor, by protecting and cultivating oneness with your wife. You started in ministry together. Finish together.[3]

FINISH STRONG

Persevering in ministry doesn't happen without commitment and effort. Paul urges men in ministry to "persist in this" (1 Tim 4:16). "Persist" can be translated "persevere." The verb tense indicates constant activity: Keep on persevering.

"In this" is plural—"in these things" (NASB)—and refers to both the personal practices ("yourself") and the teaching responsibilities ("the teaching") described in the preceding verses. Paul prodded Timothy, "Don't let these practices drop. Persevere in them."

When you're a new pastor, watch yourself in these areas. When your ministry is prospering, be especially careful. When ministry is painful, pay close attention to your personal life. When the day comes that you look back over decades of ministry, renew your commitment to guard your heart all the way to the end. Guard your integrity to have a persevering ministry.

---

3. See chapter 13 on "Companionship in a Ministry Marriage" for more thorough content on developing oneness in your marriage.

Start strong. Stay strong. Finish strong. Don't let up. Stay on guard. Watch yourself until your ministry work is complete and you're greeted, "Well done."

REFLECT AND DISCUSS

1. Are there any ways thinking or acting immaturely might affect your longevity in ministry? How should you address these?

2. In what areas of your outward life are you vulnerable to damaging your integrity? What about your inner life? How should you address these?

3. How do you guard your moral purity? Are there any other steps you should take?

PART 3

CRITICAL AREAS

A PASTOR'S ANTIDOTE FOR UNWORTHINESS

"FEED MY SHEEP"

These words were spoken in a beautiful outdoor setting. Early morning air. The lake's glassy surface reflecting the pink edges of sunrise in the eastern sky. Warm fire crackling on the shore, the satisfaction of a full stomach, the comfort of friends. But for one man, the pleasure of these circumstances was overshadowed by deep, aching regret.

Peter's self-preserving impulse came back to bite him hard as the One he had denied served him a cooked breakfast, then went right for the heart.

The familiar smell of woodsmoke triggered a painful memory—his refusal to be associated with the arrested Galilean. He could not unsay those words, "I do not know the man" (Matt 27:72). Now here the friend he abandoned stood face-to-face, asking a strange question. Not, "Why did you deny me?" but, "Do you love me?" (John 21:15).

The Greek word for "charcoal fire" is used in two places in the New Testament. John included the fire in his depiction of Jesus with the disciples in John 21:9. The other setting is outside the high priest's house where Peter and others stayed warm while Jesus was interrogated inside: "And when they had kindled a fire in the middle of the courtyard and sat down together, Peter sat down among them" (Luke 22:55).

There by that fire, Peter lied. He swore. He refused to be connected to Jesus. Then regret tore him up inside. He "wept bitterly" (Luke 22:62).

Now his friend is dead. But then . . . risen! And the message, "He is going before you to Galilee; there you will see him" (Matt 28:7).

Dread, but anticipation. Peter would face Jesus. What would He say?

"Catching anything boys? Try the other side of the boat!"

"It is the Lord!"

"Come have breakfast." A fire.

"Peter, do you love me?"

If the fire was not enough to signal to Peter this was an opportunity to move back toward Jesus, to right the wrong, then the question Jesus asked—three times!—was. Jesus laid out a path of restoration for Peter. The first step, really the one big step, was not mere acknowledgment or association, but loyal devotion—"Do you love me?"

Peter's heart hurt at what he had done to Jesus—"Peter was grieved" (John 21:17)—but he leaped at the opportunity to make it right, to renounce disloyalty and declare love. "Yes, Lord; you know that I love you" (John 21:15). Jesus could have justly disowned Peter. But instead He offered Peter the opportunity to declare his loyal love once and for all time, and to follow Jesus through his life, to the death. What grace.

Here, my pastor friend, is something we must all remember. Like Peter, we are in ministry, not by virtue of any goodness in us, but because of God's magnanimous grace.

Not only at the time of our salvation, but again and again, we realize we don't deserve the position we are in, that of being right with God. Those who are appointed to ministry are frequently reminded of this fact. Who are we, not only to benefit from God's grace ourselves, but to be messengers of that grace to others, and to have a leadership role in God's work?

We remember the ways we have disappointed our Lord. We feel unworthy to fellowship with Him, much less to represent Him in ministry. But His grace superabundantly exceeds our sin. This grace is not just for your people—it is for you. "Now the law came in to increase the trespass, but where sin increased, grace abounded all the more, so that, as sin reigned in death, grace also might reign through righteousness leading to eternal life through Jesus Christ our Lord" (Rom 5:20–21). Grace reigns in your life!

Jesus's instruction to Peter is His great commission to every pastor: "Feed my lambs" (John 21:15). Three times He asked Peter, "Do you love me?" Three times Peter affirmed his love. Three times Jesus directed Peter what to do next. Jesus restored Peter to fellowship, then commissioned him to ministry. "Tend my sheep" (v. 16). "Feed my sheep" (v. 17).

The instruction "Feed my sheep" was referenced by the apostle Paul when he charged the Ephesian pastors as recorded in Acts 20:28: "Be on guard for yourselves and for all the flock, among which the Holy Spirit has made you overseers, to shepherd the church of God which He purchased with His own blood" (NASB).

Peter himself applied the same instruction to pastors in 1 Peter 5:2: "Shepherd the flock of God that is among you."

In each case, the privilege of filling the role of shepherd—pastor—is in view. Pastors are not self-made, but Spirit-made (Acts 20:28). And we are not owners or masters. We care for "the church of God which he obtained with his own blood" (Acts 20:28), the "flock of God" (1 Pet 5:2). Those terms marking out God's ownership and authority are reminders that pastors are in their positions not by right, but by God's gracious choice.

ANTIDOTE FOR UNWORTHINESS

Is there a connection between Peter's conversation with Jesus on the shore of the Sea of Galilee and your position as a pastor today? Here's what I see: God's grace in saving you and putting you in ministry is the antidote for unworthiness. [1]

During my twenty-five years as a pastor, I think I doubted my ability and right to care for souls every day. Who am I to tell people how to live? Memories of past sins and the sharp consciousness of present, daily struggles eroded my confidence for ministering to others. Do you experience this?

---

1. Some sin patterns do disqualify a man from pastoral ministry (see 1 Timothy 3 and Titus 1). I am referring to a general sense of unworthiness based on feelings of guilt over non-disqualifying sins that are already forgiven by God.

Satan, the accuser, reminds us regularly of our unworthiness. But the ever-cleansing blood of Christ removes its basis. The great transaction of justification places us into a right relationship with God. "Therefore, since we have been justified by faith, we have peace with God through our Lord Jesus Christ. Through him we have also obtained access by faith into this grace in which we stand, and we rejoice in hope of the glory of God" (Rom 5:1–2).

Justified pastor friend, you have peace with God. You have access to God. You stand in grace! You have hope as your source of joy. You were unworthy, but you are made worthy in Jesus Christ.

GRACE FOR MINISTRY

Your role and work as a pastor are yours through God's grace. Consider three texts of Scripture that reveal the grace basis for ministry.

Ephesians 4:7 declares that "grace was given to each one of us according to the measure of Christ's gift." The thought continues in verse 8, "[Christ] gave gifts to men." Then Paul links these gifts that flow from God's grace to the position you hold in the church—"And he gave . . . the shepherds and teachers, to equip the saints for the work of ministry, for building up the body of Christ" (vv. 11–12). Are you unworthy to hold the office of pastor? Yes! But God is gracious!

First Peter 4:10 also reveals that God's grace is the source of our abilities and opportunities to serve in the church: "As each has received a gift, use it to serve one another, as good stewards of God's varied grace." Then your role as a speaker of truth is identified: "Whoever speaks, as one who speaks oracles of God" (v. 11). Are you unworthy to preach? Of course. But God has graciously enlisted and enabled you to speak for Him.

First Timothy 1:12–17 reveals Paul's overwhelming sense of unworthiness for ministry. His reassurance? "The grace of our Lord overflowed for me with the faith and love that are in Christ Jesus" (v. 14). You and I can say with Paul, "By the grace of God I am what I am, and his grace toward me was not in vain" (1 Cor 15:10).

Take a few minutes and receive these truths as reassurances from God Himself to you. Allow them to purge out shame, doubt, guilt, regret, and paralyzing feelings of unworthiness.

- I am justified by God's free favor through my faith in the substitutionary death and victorious resurrection of Jesus Christ the Lord.

- I am right with God. My right standing with God is objective truth. Formerly an enemy, I am officially at peace with God.

- I was unworthy to draw near to God myself, even less worthy to represent Him to others. But now I stand in grace. I am in God's favor. My past performance did not earn God's favor. My present performance does not keep me in God's favor. My position in God's favor is secure.

- God's gracious provision for me includes my place in the body of Christ. His free, unmerited and unmeritable favor that provided me with salvation (Eph 2:8–9) also granted my role as a pastor (Eph 4:7–8, 11–12).

- I am a pastor by the grace of God. I am humbly grateful and will move forward in confidence, not in my worthiness, but in God's sovereign choice and limitless grace.

Allow these truths to saturate your soul, fill your mind, and channel your thoughts. Review them regularly. Reflect them to God in prayers of thanksgiving. Speak them to your own soul. Step into your pulpit, drive to that visit, enter your next counseling appointment, in grace-based confidence.

Paul gratefully acknowledged he was in ministry only by God's grace.

> I thank him who has given me strength, Christ Jesus our Lord, because he judged me faithful, appointing me to his service, though formerly I was a blasphemer, persecutor, and insolent opponent.

But I received mercy because I had acted ignorantly in unbelief, and the grace of our Lord overflowed for me with the faith and love that are in Christ Jesus.

The saying is trustworthy and deserving of full acceptance, that Christ Jesus came into the world to save sinners, of whom I am the foremost. But I received mercy for this reason, that in me, as the foremost, Jesus Christ might display his perfect patience as an example to those who were to believe in him for eternal life.

To the King of the ages, immortal, invisible, the only God, be honor and glory forever and ever. Amen. (1 Tim 1:12–17)

Every leader serves in Christ's church-building work because of God's overflowing grace.

Grace doesn't deny our unworthiness. It overpowers it. It redirects the focus from us to God. Because of our unworthiness, Jesus can display His faithfulness, love, and patience. We and all who know us can exclaim, "To Him be the glory forever and ever."

So push aside those feelings of unworthiness, and go take care of your sheep.

CHAPTER SIX

REFLECT AND DISCUSS

1. What is surprising about the way Jesus interacted with Peter? What do you learn of the ways of Christ from this interaction?

2. When do you feel unworthy for ministry?

3. Select two to three reassurances from God that you find especially helpful. Say them out loud. Give thanks to God for them. Develop a means of reminding yourself of them when you are feeling unworthy for any part of your ministry work.

CHAPTER SEVEN

MINISTRY STRESS RELIEF

Did you know there is an American Institute of Stress? It's true. Their website offers this definition: Stress is "a condition or feeling experienced when a person perceives that demands exceed the personal and social resources the individual is able to mobilize."[1] I think of stress as feeling pressured, but I hadn't realized the source of that pressure until I read their definition. I feel stressed when I'm facing more than I can handle. The demands on me are greater than the physical or emotional energy, mental capacity, or spiritual wisdom that I can muster.

People who don't understand ministry might think it's a low-stress job, but you and I know better. The stress index is often high. And when it isn't, a single text message, email, or phone call can escalate it quickly. I would say most if not all pastors feel significant stress every day.

I surveyed some pastor friends with this question: What causes you stress in ministry? You can probably identify with many of their answers.

- Preparing to preach, the weekly responsibility of preaching, handling the eternal Word of God.

- Demands on time, having too much to do for the time available. If doing everything necessary for ministry, the result is neglecting family. If focusing on family, the result is neglecting ministry. Pastoring bivocationally compounds these factors.

---

1. "What is Stress?" Stress.org, https://www.stress.org/what-is-stress/.

- Dealing with conflicts in the church

- Expectations—a pastor's self-imposed expectations and the expectations (real or perceived) of others

- Administrative tasks

- Gossip and criticism

These are but a few of the stressful elements of ministry that a pastor faces regularly. I don't need to convince you: ministry is stressful.

To encourage you, I want to walk through a passage of Scripture written by a man who experienced a severe degree of stress. Paul, follower of Jesus, church founder, premiere missionary, and author of Scripture, almost broke under the weight of responsibility on him and hostility against him. We can identify with the causes of stress Paul faced and find help in the sources of relief he found. Let's spend a few minutes together in 2 Corinthians chapters 1 to 3.

CAUSES OF STRESS

From 2 Corinthians 3:1 we can infer that Paul's authority and ability to carry out his calling and assignment were being challenged: "Are we beginning to commend ourselves again? Or do we need, as some do, letters of recommendation to you, or from you?"

Opponents to Paul and to the gospel were influencing those to whom he was ministering. We face similar questions, whether from other people or from within ourselves: "Are you qualified? What makes you think you are capable? What are you even doing here?"

Intense Pressure

Let's look a little more closely at what caused Paul's stress. Back in 2 Corinthians 1:8 he referred to "the affliction we experienced in Asia." The word "affliction" refers to being pressed or crushed. It is used of crushing grapes for juice and is used in the New Testament of suffering, persecution, and hostility associated with the end times, poverty, sickness, fear, and death.

Paul also described himself as "burdened beyond our strength." Burdened means weighed down with sorrow, discouragement, pressure, or problems, whether your own or others'.

So the "affliction in Asia" caused Paul to be "burdened beyond our strength." We don't know what the difficulty in Asia was—possibly plots and attempts to kill him, being beaten with thirty-nine lashes (2 Cor 11:24), some other persecution, or a physical illness. Whatever it was, Paul was traumatized by it.

How bad was it? Paul was not using hyperbole when he described himself as "so utterly burdened beyond our strength that we despaired of life itself" (2 Cor 1:8). He was like the proverbial camel whose back finally cracked under the cumulative weight of thousands of pieces of straw.

Despaired means to be utterly at loss, destitute of resources, having lost hope, and at the point of giving up. The Greek word means there is no exit available, no way out!

When the pressure on you is more than you can bear, you can't see a path forward, and there's no way out, the result is total despair. And that is where many pastors find themselves. I have felt it myself and heard other pastors use that dark word—*despair.*

If you thought it couldn't get any worse, Paul goes down another level—"despaired of life itself" (2 Cor 1:8). This has several possible meanings. It could be that Paul knew death was a possibility; persecutors were plotting to take his life. It could mean he thought the only escape from the unbearable stress he felt was death. And it could even mean Paul wished it were so—that his life would end so the suffering would too.

Can Christians get to this low point? Yes. Pressure, stress, discouragement, depression, guilt, and hopelessness can drive even one of God's own to despair. Unless someone introduces hope, a pastor might spiral downward and consider death as the only escape.

Misunderstanding and Misrepresentation

A specific kind of pressure comes in the form of being misunderstood. Evidently Paul had changed his travel plans, and his opponents in Corinth put their spin on it, accusing Paul of being unreliable. He attempted to explain himself in 2 Corinthians 1:13–18. He said, "I hope you will fully understand" (v. 13).

One of the most intense pressures I've experienced is when attempting to lead the church through stages of change. Our pastoral team and I endeavored to provide a biblical basis for the changes, communicate clearly, answer all questions, and take careful steps rather than implement changes abruptly. Even so, there were a few individuals who misunderstood our motives and vocally misrepresented the reasons for the steps we were taking as a church. Thankfully it was only a few, but it doesn't take much to stir up a pastor's anxious heart.

Addressing Sin

If you're familiar with Paul's work with the Corinthians, you know he had to address serious moral sin in the church (1 Cor 5:1–5). Pastors know this can be extremely stressful. In 2 Corinthians 2:1, Paul refers to his action as a "painful visit" and in verse 2 as "caus[ing] you pain." He also confronted them about divisiveness, a lack of financial giving, thoughtlessness about the Lord's Supper, and conflict over issues of conscience.

There are times we have to take hard steps with people we love. Especially when it involves deep moral sin, the anguish is two-fold, as we bring discomfort into their lives and feel it in our own hearts as well.

Spiritual Warfare

The role of Satan comes into view when Paul cautions the Corinthians about being "outwitted by Satan; for we are not ignorant of his devices" (2 Cor 2:11). This caution is in the context of admonishing them not to withhold forgiveness from a repentant fellow church member. Satan strategizes how to exploit Christians' failures and disrupt church unity.

He is still as active today as he was then. He is the accuser, and he specializes in pitting people against each other. Who are we to battle Satan? The demand of spiritual warfare is greater than our personal resources to do battle, resulting in stress.

Missed Fellowship

"My spirit was not at rest" is how Paul described his reaction to his ministry associate, Titus, not showing up for their agreed on rendezvous (2 Cor 2:13). It seems Paul had planned a ministry trip to Troas that did not materialize due to Titus not being there to meet him. He missed an opportunity for fellowship with his friend, and his plans were frustrated. The result was unrest in his mind and heart, which we might equate with some form of stress.

Ministry in an isolated place and the disappointment of not having ministry associates or confidantes to share the burden with you can have the same effect—unrest in your spirit.

Successful Ministry

It may sound strange, but times when ministry is thriving can produce stress. Paul described his successful gospel work as "Christ . . . through us spread[ing] the fragrance of the knowledge of him everywhere" (2 Cor 2:14). Your church may experience seasons of expansion and multiplication that exceed your natural ability to manage, resulting in the feeling of being overwhelmed.

Paul's famous self-disclosure in 2 Corinthians 11:28 legitimizes the feeling you and I have at times—"the daily pressure on me of my anxiety for all the churches." What a success story—the number of churches Paul planted and assisted! With success comes stress.

Religious Merchandisers

Then, as now, many captivating messages and personalities influenced church members' minds and hearts, being motivated not by love but by greed—"peddlers of God's word" (2 Cor 2:17). How does one faithful pastor compete with the media machine cranking out books, blogs, and podcasts, many of which may lead people astray, or at least divert their attention and energy from their own local church?

One or a number of these factors Paul experienced may be sources of stress in your ministry. The demands on your time, energy, and expertise exceed your capacity to meet them, and you cry, like Paul, "Who is sufficient for these things?" (2 Cor 2:16). This can be a very vulnerable place for a pastor. A. T. Robertson observes, "The real difficulties and problems of the ministry are magnified out of all proportion to the facts. In such a case a minister is in jeopardy. He is in danger of becoming bitter toward the world, jealous of other ministers, disgusted with his own task. Thus he will lose his compass and drift out to sea."[2]

But our insufficiency can also point us to find strength and hope in sources outside of ourselves. Thankfully Paul found relief and so can we.

RELIEF FROM REALIZING THE EXTENT OF YOUR INFLUENCE

When you are overwhelmed, you can lose sight of the impact you are having through your preaching, your spiritual care, and your leadership. Sometimes the Lord graciously gives you a glimpse of the extent of your influence, and it can be very encouraging.

Paul called the Corinthians "our letter of recommendation, written on our hearts, to be known and read by all . . . a letter from Christ delivered by us, written not with ink but with the Spirit of the living God" (2 Cor 3:2–3). These believers were being pushed to question Paul's credibility. But they themselves were the best evidence of the legitimacy and success of his ministry! His influence left the imprint of Christ on their lives for all to see. Paul was the instrument—"delivered by us." "The change of heart

---

2. A. T. Robertson, *The Glory of the Ministry* (Wipf and Stock Publishers, 1998), 23–24. I highly recommend this rich and personal exposition of 2 Corinthians 2–6, written for the express purpose of encouraging pastors.

that the Corinthian believers had experienced as a result of Paul's ministry among them was proof inescapable of its fulfillment."[3]

Our influence is measured not primarily by what we see but by the unseen work of God in hearts which eventually works its way out into the lives of the people we touch. Paul describes this work as "the Spirit of the living God, not on tablets of stone but on tablets of human hearts" (v. 3). We reach people on a spiritual level, and it takes time for it to become visible in their lives.

You have more influence than you realize. What you see now is not a measure of your success. Growth is often incremental and progressive, not sudden and drastic. In fact, you may not know the extent of your influence until years later, even after you leave a ministry. This reality can help you keep going when the stress levels are high and you're wondering if it's worth it. Let me share a few examples.

Twenty years ago I left the church I had pastored for just over nine years. Recently I was back for an anniversary service. A couple approached me and related a story. He was attending the church, and his wife was not a believer. He recounted that he had met with me to tell me what his wife was doing wrong and get my advice on how to get her to change.

Now this next part I didn't remember, but here's what he said. I told him I didn't want to hear what she was doing wrong. I instructed him to give her a blank piece of paper and have her write down how he could love her better. So he did. And they told me the rest of their story. His wife saw how his life showed the love of God, and she trusted Christ and was saved! What I could have viewed as a stressful counseling situation turned into an opportunity for eternal impact on that couple and their family.

The current pastor of a thriving church plant attended the church where I pastored while he was a college student. He recounted recently how my expository approach while preaching through the book of Romans awakened a desire in him to learn to preach God's Word in a similar way. I had

---

3. Philip E. Hughes, *The Second Epistle to the Corinthians*, The New International Commentary on the New Testament (Wm. B. Eerdmans Publishing Company, 1962), 89.

no idea at the time that my preaching was not only impacting the present lives of the people in front of me, but that it was shaping a young man's view of preaching and would be formative in his future ministry.

When I was a youth pastor, my wife taught the senior high girls Sunday school class. Just a few years ago (almost thirty years later), she received a message from a young lady who had been in our youth group. We had dinner with her, and she related this story.

She was in junior high when Faith was teaching the senior high class. One Sunday morning she and a friend snuck out of their junior high class and into Faith's class. An adult youth sponsor was about to send them back, but Faith told her it was okay, they could stay. Over dinner, she told my wife that the way she was treated in that moment made a huge impact on her and helped her view of church and God's work in her life. Faith did not even remember the incident. Just a little flexibility and gentleness on her part had made a difference in this girl's life.

When ministry is stressful, remember, the people you impact are "letter[s] of Christ." God is using you to imprint the character of Christ on their hearts. We are inadequate, but He uses us as His instruments.

RELIEF FROM CONSIDERING THE OBJECT OF YOUR CONFIDENCE

Stressful circumstances reveal what we're trusting in. It's true that we are inadequate for spiritual ministry. But if we are doing the ministry to which God has called us, then we can make a conscious choice to trust Him for whatever we need to accomplish it.

Paul declared, "Such is the confidence that we have through Christ toward God" (2 Cor 3:4). The first Greek word in this sentence, *de*, signifies a different or unexpected direction of thought and could be translated *yet* or *but*.

And he says "we have" this confidence—literally "we are continually having." Confidence is defined as "to believe in something or someone to the extent of placing reliance or trust in or on—'to rely on, to trust in, to depend on, to have complete confidence in.'" [4] The word "comes from the same Greek root as faith, trust, believe (*peithō* and *pistis, pisteuō*). It basically means trust, confidence, or reliance." [5]

The word such indicates this kind of confidence. He is referring to what he just described in verses two and three—the confidence that comes from knowing he is an instrument in Christ's work. And he had this confidence "through Christ." Through Christ our mediator our imperfect efforts are acceptable to God, our inadequate efforts are enabled by God, our sin-tainted offerings of service are made presentable to God. And this confidence is "toward God"—ultimately in Him alone.

What was true for Paul is true for us as well. The overwhelming demands of ministry prompt us to renew our complete reliance on God, knowing our meager efforts are rendered pleasing to Him through the mediation of our high priest who intercedes for us, Christ our Savior.

RELIEF FROM UNDERSTANDING THE SOURCE OF YOUR SUFFICIENCY

We can be confident because we understand the source of our sufficiency. As with Paul, stress reminds us we are insufficient—"Not that we are sufficient in ourselves to claim anything as coming from us" (2 Cor 3:5). And we know that God is the all-sufficient one—"our sufficiency is from God." One of God's Old Testament names, *El Shaddai*, was sometimes interpreted as "the Sufficient One." Possibly Paul had that Hebrew understanding in mind here—"Our sufficiency comes from the Sufficient One." [6]

---

4. J. P. Louw and E. A. Nida (1996). *Greek-English Lexicon of the New Testament: Based on Semantic Domains* (electronic ed. of the 2nd edition, New York: United Bible Societies, 1:375.

5. R. J. Utley, *Paul's Letters to a Troubled Church: I and II Corinthians*, Study Guide Commentary Series New Testament, (Bible Lessons International, 2002), 6:221.

6. Hughes, 93.

Paul looked back to his conversion and call to ministry as the time when God equipped him for these heavy responsibilities and circumstances. "Who has made us sufficient" (v. 6) is an aorist tense verb, pointing back to a definite occasion. This probably links to Paul's testimony in 1 Timothy 1:12, "who has given me strength (aorist tense) . . . appointing me to his service."[7]

The summary of all of this is God "has made us sufficient to be ministers of the new covenant" (2 Cor 3:6). You are adequate because God made you adequate. Just as God made Paul adequate for his daunting ministry work, He does for you and me as well.

Recently I became interested in fountain pens. I've made several messes with ink leaking everywhere, smudging my paper and staining my hands. With practice, I've become more adept. There are those who wield such an instrument with artistic skill, producing pages that not only inform and communicate, but evidence a master's hand.

The Holy Spirit is inscribing the character of Christ on the hearts of your people. You are His pen. Your part is to trust Him and allow Him to minister through you.

True, Paul had a unique ministry as an apostle and was specially used by God in the first phase of spreading the gospel and establishing churches. But we are continuing the work he began, serving the same church being built by Christ, indwelt and empowered by the same Spirit, and sharing the same gospel message.

Our instinctive answer to the question "Who is sufficient for these things?" (2 Cor 2:16) is "No one, especially not me!" But the correct answer is "I am, because God has made me so. In Him, I am qualified for the work and adequate for the task."

---

7. Ibid.

REFLECT AND DISCUSS

1. You feel stress when the demands on you are greater than your physical or emotional energy, mental capacity, or spiritual wisdom. What is causing you stress right now?

2. Do any of Paul's sources of stress from 2 Corinthians 1— 3 sound like your experience? Which ones, and how are they relevant to you?

3. Do any of Paul's sources of relief from stress help you? Which ones, and how can you apply them to your situation?

ACTION STEPS FOR OVERCOMING DISCOURAGEMENT

Pastors grow discouraged. It goes with the territory. Some battle it more than others. You are not alone. Listen to the words of a fellow pastor and see if you identify with his feelings of inadequacy and the resulting discouragement:

> No day passes without strong temptation to give up this work—this temptation appeals to me on the ground that I am not fitted for pastoral work; writing sermons is often the hardest labour to me, visiting is terrible. I often stand before a door unable to ring or knock—sometimes I have gone away without entering. A lowness of spirit that it costs me a great deal to throw off is the consequence of this, and a real doubt whether it would not be better for myself and all whom it may concern that I should at once look for some other work that I could overtake.[1]

The circumstances that produce discouragement are numerous. I won't try to list them, but, brothers, we are on common ground. I have lan-

---

1. Robertson, 27–28, quoting from the March 8, 1860 diary of Marcus Dods, minister in the Free Church of Scotland (1834–1900).

guished there, and I have experienced the grace of God helping me. During one low season I read through 2 Timothy several times and made a list of "things to do" for a discouraged pastor.

I think one of the purposes for this letter from Paul was to encourage Timothy when he was down. Why? Here are some clues.

Paul said in 2 Timothy 1:4 that he was aware of Timothy's tears. Tears are part of ministry! I remember saying to my wife one time, "What other profession makes you cry?" Paul spoke of his own tears in Acts 20:19, 31 and 2 Corinthians 2:4 ("many tears").

Other clues to Paul's intent to encourage Timothy include his acknowledgment of the fear Timothy was experiencing (2 Tim 1:7). In verse 8 and following, Paul challenged Timothy to not let suffering for Christ get him down. In 1:13 he tells Timothy to "hold fast"; in 2:1 to "be strong"; in 2:3 to "endure hardship"; in 3:14 to "continue"; and in 4:5 to "fulfill your ministry" (NKJV). Some commentaries say he wasn't necessarily discouraged, but potentially could be. If he was discouraged, Paul wanted to encourage him. If he wasn't, Paul anticipated he might be in the future.

It's important to recognize these are grace-empowered actions as Paul emphasized in 2:1: "Be strengthened by the grace that is in Christ Jesus." God can strengthen us to take action when we are discouraged.

WHAT TO DO WHEN YOU'RE DOWN

Rekindle the Fire

"Fan into flame the gift of God, which is in you through the laying on of my hands" (2 Tim 1:6).

When you are discouraged, you may question your ministry effectiveness and possibly even your calling. It helps to review your initial calling to ministry and to remember that God has gifted you in specific ways to build and bless His church.

"Fan into flame" means rekindle the fire or make the fire alive again. "The gift of God which is in you through the laying on of my hands" probably refers to Timothy's calling and gift for ministry as a preacher and church leader. His calling was recognized by "the body of elders" (1 Tim 4:14 NIV) and Paul—"my hands" (2 Tim 1:6); Paul was saying, "Timothy, God called you, and I helped ordain you!"

My adult children gave me a meat smoker for Father's Day a few years ago. I've learned to make mouth-watering ribs, savory beef brisket, and the most flavorful Thanksgiving turkey ever. One of the tricks, since it's a charcoal and wood smoker, not electric, is to keep the temperature steady. Smoked meat cooks best "low and slow." Around 225 degrees is optimal. One time I did not use enough charcoal when I started the fire and the temperature in the smoker dropped to 175. I lit some fresh charcoal briquets in my chimney starter where they could heat up fast, then added the red-hot coals to the smoldering pile in the bottom of the smoker. The temperature escalated to the required level, and we enjoyed the delicious outcome.

Paul told Timothy to get his fire going again! Is this what you need? Here are a few actions I jotted down that can rekindle your fire.

- Remember God's initial calling on your life. Was there Scripture He used? People who encouraged you? Who was at your ordination? If you have a certificate, look at the names and remember their influence on your life. Call one of them up! "Every Christian minister needs at times to return to the inspiration of his ordination, to be reminded not only of the greatness of his calling, but also of the adequacy of the divine grace which enables him to perform it."[2]

- Remind yourself of what your gifts are and how God has used them to build and bless His church. Churches go through seasons of life and growth. God uses different kinds of leaders during those stages. He may be using you

---

2. Donald Guthrie, *The Pastoral Epistles*, Tyndale New Testament Commentary, (IVP Academic, 2009), 14:126.

in ways you don't realize. Complete what God brought you there to do. Possibly you reach a point when you step away from a ministry when it is the right time, and the church thrives under a new pastor. Rejoice in the growth of the body and that God used you to accomplish what He intended in that stage of its growth.

- Review how God led you to your current place of ministry. I know for me, there were circumstances, key passages of Scripture, and intense seasons of prayer and seeking God's direction that led to our move to each ministry. It's helpful to remember the way God worked to get you there when you go through tough times.

- Recommit yourself to living out your calling, to using your gifts for building and blessing the church, and to complete dependence on God, the Spirit, in using your gifts. Take time to pray and express your response to God's grace at work in your life, your dependence on Him, and your resolve to fulfill your ministry in the strength He gives.

See Gospel Purpose in Your Pain

We find another grace-empowered action to take when discouraged in 2 Timothy 1:8–11: "Therefore do not be ashamed of the testimony about our Lord, nor of me his prisoner, but share in the suffering for the gospel by the power of God."

Paul himself experienced hardship and suffering in ministry. He encouraged Timothy and took courage himself from the gospel—the good news that Jesus, God's Son, died for our sins and rose again, and those who trust Jesus alone for salvation will know God and live with Him forever.

Look at two examples Paul gave of seeing painful experiences through the gospel lens. The first example is himself. He reminded Timothy that his suffering was "for the gospel" (v. 8) and that God "has saved us and called us to a holy calling . . . because of His own purpose and grace" (v. 9). Jesus "abolished death and brought life and immortality to light through the gospel, for which I was appointed a preacher . . . which is why I suffer as I do. But I am not ashamed" (vv. 11–12). And he tells Timothy not to be ashamed either (v. 8). Paul suffered, but he knew there was gospel purpose for his painful experiences.

The second example is a man named Onesiphorus. He could have been embarrassed by his association with Paul the prisoner, but instead, he "was not ashamed of my chains" (v. 16). He ministered to Paul regardless of the stigma associated with Paul's status as a prisoner. Because Paul was being held as a result of his gospel work, there was gospel-driven purpose in Onesiphorus's efforts on Paul's behalf.

Shame and embarrassment come from being overly-sensitive to the hardship and hostility that go with gospel ministry. Sometimes our emotions control our decisions, including how we view ministry and the people in it. Paul challenged Timothy not to be ruled by emotion but to be governed by the gospel.

When we're down, we tend to make decisions based on emotional discouragement and hurt rather than on gospel confidence, hope, and calling. Problems loom large in our minds, and we lose sight of the gospel cause and how God is using us in it. Discouraged pastors should review the gospel and take heart from its life-transforming impact in our own lives and the people we minister to. Refuse to view your ministry through an emotional lens. Instead, look at it through the lens of the gospel.

Looking back over the years God gave me in pastoral ministry, many examples of the life-transforming impact of the gospel come to mind. One that stands out is a family who was invited to our church by one of our members. They had numerous struggles, but the most obvious was that the husband was addicted to crack cocaine. His addiction was destroying their marriage, draining their finances, and doing serious damage to his body and mind. He wanted help, so we began to meet early in the morning once a week at McDonalds. He trusted Christ to save him, and I guided him through reading and meditating on key passages of Scripture. He grew, had times of victory and occasions of failure, then was finally delivered from bondage to that enslaving addiction.

Even though there were discouraging situations and people who didn't respond as positively to the gospel, that man's life and family were transformed, and I was greatly encouraged by seeing firsthand the power of the Word of God in one person's life.

When you're discouraged, think of people you've influenced toward Christ. Remember those you've discipled and counseled, in whose lives the gospel has made the difference. Review your own salvation—the people and circumstances who influenced you, and the wonderful fact that you are saved from hell to fellowship with God forever and to serve Him with your life.

I think it can also be helpful to think of your fellow Christians who face real persecution. They could easily be discouraged, but by God's grace they view their hardship through the lens of the gospel. They know that opposition is normal for genuine Christians, and rather than give up, they remain faithful to the end.

I once participated in an ordination council in India. The pastors on the council asked the candidate many of the usual theological questions I'm used to hearing in that setting. Then I heard a question I haven't heard before or since: "What will you do when persecution comes?" Persecution for those believers is assumed. I'll never forget his answer: "I will be faithful to the death." Oh for grace to keep my problems in perspective.

Stay on Message

"Follow the pattern of the sound words that you have heard from me, in the faith and love which are in Christ Jesus" (2 Tim 1:13–14). "The pattern" refers to what Paul himself had taught that was an example for Timothy's teaching ministry. "Sound words" describe preaching and teaching that fully represent truth without adding extraneous ideas or omitting vital elements. "Follow" is a present active verb meaning to possess—"stay in possession" is another way to say it.

A point guard dribbling down court with a defender tightly guarding him will keep his body between his opponent and the ball. If he stops and picks up the ball, he will keep a tight grip and hold it close so it won't be slapped away. He protects the ball so his team will stay in possession and have the opportunity to score. In the same way, a pastor is diligent to stay in possession of the truth of God's Word, not allowing pressing circumstances to separate him from the message vital to the life of the church.

"In the faith and love that are in Christ Jesus" (v. 13) describes the manner in which he is to remain steadfastly committed to the truth. It is not merely a duty, but springs out of our faith in Christ and our love for Christ. Or "love" may refer to our love for the people we minister to. Rather than allowing the pressures of ministry and problems with people to callous our hearts, we maintain genuine concern for our flock and share the word with gentleness and care.

When people are opposing you, or circumstances are weighing on you, it's important to keep preaching and teaching the truth. One temptation might be to adjust the message to please people. The other tendency might be to preach reactively, venting about issues that frustrate or discourage you.

There's certainly a place for honesty, expressing concerns, and addressing issues pertinent to the life of the church. But the discouraged pastor should be careful to stay on center. Keep truth central. Resist the temptation to modify the message to fit current fads, to please influential people, to avoid controversy, or to vent anger or resentment.

When everything else seems uncertain, you can go to God's Word, week after week, to nourish your own soul and to feed the flock of God. Hold on to this. Keep doing this. Do it this week, and the next, and the next . . .

Bless Your Encouragers

The number of names Paul uses in 2 Timothy is remarkable. Some are people who hurt him in very personal ways. Others encouraged and helped him. These encouragers had great impact on the state of Paul's mind and spirit. Look at the names and what Paul says about them in 2 Timothy 1:15–18.

"All who are in Asia have turned away from me, among whom are Phygellus and Hermogenes." Wow! A bunch of people abandoned Paul, and he names two of them. I know we should usually try to avoid taking it personally when people leave. But Paul's response seems very personal—they "turned away from me!"

Pastor, do you ever see images of people in your head when your mind drifts, when you're feeling discouraged, when you're tossing and turning at night—the faces of people who have left your church or hurt you in some way? I have, and I'm pretty sure Paul did!

But look at what he said next. "May the Lord grant mercy to the household of Onesiphorus, for he often refreshed me and was not ashamed of my chains . . . he searched for me earnestly and found me . . . and you well know all the service he rendered at Ephesus" (vv. 16–18).

Paul also had in his mind the image, name, and sweet memory of one who had really encouraged him. He reminded himself and shared with Timothy what a blessing good ol' Onesiphorus had been. Paul's heart cry for this man was that God would bless him and his family.

People who leave are one of the greatest causes of a pastor's discouragement. The natural tendency is to expend mental and emotional energy thinking negatively about them. But the people who stay, and especially the people who care for you, who take you for coffee, send you a text, tell you they're praying for you—these are "refreshers!" There are a few who seek you out, make it a point to ask how you're doing, and pray with you. A discouraged pastor will do well to think often of, and thank God for, these.

A few years ago I wrote some reflections on twenty-five years of ministry as a pastor. I recalled kinds of people for whom I am thankful. Here was my list:

- Those who love, pray for, and support me. I remember one man in particular who often reminded me, "Pastor, I pray for you every day."

- Those who suffer deeply and give testimony through their trials to the grace and goodness of God.

- Those who are steadfast and strong and have been a source of strength for me.

- Those who will do just about anything that is needed at any time.

- Those who have overcome major struggles with sin.

- The one who has stuck with me through it all "for better or for worse."

Names and faces come to mind with each of these descriptions. I encourage you to think of the people who have encouraged you in these ways, or make your own list of categories. Then, like Paul, praise the Lord for them and pray for the Lord to bless them. Bless your encouragers, and become one yourself.

Find the Strength You Need in Jesus

How do we pursue the kind of actions we're discussing in this chapter? Paul wasn't urging Timothy to be self-confident, relying on his own strength of character, skills, or resolve. He reminded Timothy there is a source of strength available to every Christian—"be strengthened by the grace that is in Christ Jesus" (2 Tim 2:1).

Generally, grace is God's favor that we don't deserve. Specifically, as it is used here, it is God's personal help for challenging responsibilities. We have access to this help in Jesus because He is "full of grace and truth" (John 1:14).

Notice the passive voice of the verb in 2 Timothy 2:1—"be strengthened." It's also present tense, indicating continual action. "In" before grace can denote "by means of." He's saying, "Keep on being strengthened by means of God's personal help that is yours in Christ." This is an ongoing work that God does in you as you continually depend on Him through every day, every week, every season of church life.

Mounce points out that Paul rarely, possibly only here, uses the article "the" before "grace." Paul is emphasizing, "The kind of strength you need can only come to you through *the* grace—the grace that is only in Christ."[3] There is only one kind of grace that *can* strengthen you, and this kind of grace *will* strengthen you. Because you have Christ, you have access to this grace.

How can we get this grace? Hebrews tells us we can simply ask for it. Because Jesus can "sympathize with our weaknesses" (Heb 4:15), He understands the overwhelming sense of inadequacy and inability that leads us to discouragement. Because He is full of grace, and because He understands our need for it, we can "come boldly to the throne of grace, that we may obtain mercy and find grace to help in time of need" (v. 16). And the promise of James 4:6 is yours—"He gives more grace . . . he gives grace to the humble."

So when you are discouraged, feeling weak, inadequate, overwhelmed, you can openly acknowledge it to your Savior and ask Him for the help you need. As He pours His grace into your life, you can face the overwhelming responsibilities, problems, decisions, and needs that are part of ministry.

Take a walk or go to a quiet place where you can freely commune with God. Tell him you're weak, faltering, and discouraged. Pour it out! Then ask your understanding Savior for grace.

Return strong. But keep going back to that place—the place where you ask for grace.

I've found a secret place of comfort and release,
A special place of healing, a quiet place of peace;
And everyone who dwells there finds rests beneath God's wings.
In the shade of His pavilion, new strength He always brings.

I find hope; I find grace
Far away from the world's embrace.

---

3. William D. Mounce, *Word Biblical Commentary: Pastoral Epistles* (Zondervan, 2000), 504.

He gives me rest; He keeps me safe
I find His strength; I seek His face
In the secret place.

With every trial He brings, my Lord will make a way
To strengthen and protect me, to help me face each day.
He leads me through the valley to draw me closer still,
Knowing even in the shadows, I find His perfect will.

I find hope; I find grace
Far away from the world's embrace.
He gives me rest; He keeps me safe;
I find His strength; I seek His face
In the secret place.[4]

A. T. Robertson captured the joy of men of God who undergo the hardest of times but receive strengthening grace from Christ.

[Paul] had his great experiences of the grace of God in Christ. No one can take them away from him. The richness of experience becomes the heritage of every servant of Christ. He can laugh at the doubts of the tyros in religious matters. Many men with great names are novices in grace. The seasoned soldier of the Cross has been through the war with Christ. By the campfire of hallowed experiences they can renew the great hours when the Son of God walked in the fiery furnace with them. These men cannot be shaken by the attacks of all the infidels in the world. No amount of ignorance on the part of the other man can make untrue the knowledge of Christ which they carry in their hearts.[5]

---

4. Jonathan Hamilton, "The Secret Place" (Majesty Music, Inc., 2006). The lyrics were written by Cheryl Reid and Ron Hamilton, members of the church I served as pastor when it was written. This song has personally encouraged me in my communion with God.

5. Robertson, *Glory of the Ministry*, 224.

Start a Men's Bible Study

"And what you have heard from me in the presence of many witnesses, entrust to faithful men who will be able to teach others also" (2 Tim 2:2).

When I get discouraged, I question my effectiveness, withdraw from people, and fall into a cycle of negative thinking about my influence on others. My thoughts focus on the people who are not receptive to my leadership.

Paul urged Timothy to do one of the simplest and most effective things a pastor can do. Select a few men who are receptive to your leadership and teaching. Get them together. Talk about the Bible or some topic that will help them grow in their personal lives and in their leadership. Do this with a view to developing and encouraging them toward being a positive influence in the lives of others—their buddies, their acquaintances, their families, or even additional study groups.

This will accomplish two things. First, it will encourage you to spend time with people who want and respond to your leadership. Their receptiveness and growth will be something positive in your ministry that will lift your heart. Second, if negative things are happening in your ministry, these men will become forces for good. They will carry the truths you discuss into conversations they have with others. They will generate positive energy in the church body.

Put a few names on paper. Pick a section of the Bible or a good book on an aspect of spiritual life and growth. Find out who's interested in getting together. Set a time frame on it—three months, six months, or a year. Get started. You'll be encouraged, and they will grow.

Soldier Up

"Share in suffering as a good soldier of Jesus Christ" (2 Tim 2:3).

Soldiers face long marches, rough terrain, lack of sleep and food, constant life-threatening danger, fierce hostility from enemies, and more. Pastors face tough conditions and hostile people too. It goes with the territory. None of us gets special treatment that protects us from the hardships of life and ministry. We shouldn't be surprised when there's hardship.

It's painful, tiring, and discouraging. It isn't pleasant or fun. Oh, yes, there are many joys in ministry. But sometimes those are overshadowed by the hard stuff. When the hardships are especially heavy or long, our tendency is to want to escape. Check out. Move on. Quit.

What are we to do? Soldier up.

The words "share in suffering" or "endure hardship" (NKJV) in this verse reflect one Greek word, συγκακοπαθέω, that means to "suffer affliction." Paul tells Timothy not to run from affliction but to suffer through it. Paul used the same word in verse 9, "for which I am **suffering**, bound with chains as a criminal."

Additionally, notice verse 10, "Therefore I **endure** everything for the sake of the elect," and verse 12, "If we **endure**, we will also reign with Him." The word used here for endure is ὑπομένω, "to remain under." We might say, "stay in"!

Yes, there is a time to depart. I think a pastor can realize he has completed what God brought him to accomplish in the life of a church. There can be another assignment ahead for him and another leader who will take his present church where it needs to go. But hardship is not the signal that your assignment is over, your work done. Sometimes you just need to stay.

Remember the Resurrection

I love this one. Paul tells Timothy, "Remember Jesus Christ, risen from the dead!" (2 Tim 2:8–10). And, I may be in chains, "but the Word of God is not bound!" He applies these wonderful, powerful truths to his own painful, discouraging situation: "Therefore I endure everything!" In your powerlessness over people, problems, and your own inadequacy, remember, Jesus rose from the dead! He is all-powerful and conquered death. Your weakness is an opportunity to experience His power. And in the end, He wins, and we will all reign with Him.

In your limitations and seeming ineffectiveness, remember, God's Word is not limited or bound. It is not chained by your circumstances, other people's hardness and apathy, or your lack of ability.

Unleash the Word! If you can do nothing else, if you are paralyzed by discouragement, insecurity, lack of direction, criticism, or consciousness of your imperfections and limitations, open the Word. Infuse it into your own heart. Exposit it into the hearing and hearts of your people. The Word is not bound. The Word works.

It *will* accomplish what God wants.

> For as the rain comes down, and the snow from heaven,
> And do not return there,
> But water the earth,
> And make it bring forth and bud,
> That it may give seed to the sower
> And bread to the eater,
> So shall My word be that goes forth from My mouth;
> It shall not return to Me void,
> But it shall accomplish what I please,
> And it shall prosper in the thing for which I sent it."

Isaiah 55:10–11 (NKJV)

Confront Problems

"Remind them of these things, and charge them before God not to quarrel about words, which does no good, but only ruins the hearers" (2 Tim 2:14).

Sometimes a pastor grows discouraged because there is disunity in the church or a lack of commitment to the core truths that we all hold in common. People can become divided over secondary or even relatively minor issues. This may be a signal to the pastor that he should speak to the church family about focusing on the fundamental truths of Scripture and on the person and work of Christ. Unaddressed problems become even bigger problems, leading to more discouragement.

Paul laid out a step-by-step process for addressing divisive people in Titus 3:1–9. First, "**Remind them** to be submissive to rulers and authorities, to be obedient, to be ready for every good work, to speak evil of no one, to avoid quarreling, to be gentle, and to show perfect courtesy toward all people" (vv. 1–2). Then, if it becomes necessary to confront individuals who are disrupting church peace, deal with those people directly. "As for a person who stirs up division, after **warning him once and then twice, have nothing more to do with him**" (Titus 3:10). This instructs us to issue two warnings to a divisive person, then remove him from the fellowship of the church.

The pastor, as shepherd, must address the one or few who are causing division for the sake of the whole flock. This truth has helped me. I may have to deal with a very difficult situation with one person or address an issue within the church body for the good of the whole church. That's what a shepherd does.

Work Hard, Not to Please People but God

"Do your best to present yourself to God as one approved, a worker who has no need to be ashamed, rightly handling the word of truth" (2 Tim 2:15).

A hurting pastor may craft his sermons to appease his critics. He must be motivated to please God first. His responsibility is not primarily to get man's approval on his study and delivery of the Word, but God's. He should always be open to suggestions about how to improve his preaching but not be unduly influenced by what others think. As stated before, the Word is the primary agent through which God does His work in the life of the church.

When you're down, keep studying the Word diligently. Rather than allowing yourself to be distracted by hard circumstances or hostile people, pour energy into feeding the hungry sheep with the nourishing food of the Word, and recalibrate your heart's motivation to the highest level—bringing glory to God.

Guard Against Temptation to Indulge in Sensual Pleasure

"So flee youthful passions and pursue righteousness, faith, love, and peace, along with those who call on the Lord from a pure heart" (2 Tim 2:22).

We tend to look for comfort in sensual pleasure when we're hurting or discouraged. We may have been exposed to something when younger ("youthful") that created an appetite that can still be aroused later in life, especially during times of pressure and pain. Food, alcohol, pornography, tobacco, remembering and reliving an immoral relationship—these can become temptations when we're down. Also, we become susceptible to acting in pride, following selfish ambition, and responding to people in anger. In the power of the Spirit and the grace of Jesus Christ, turn away from these. Do not be controlled by them.

Instead pursue godly character and practices and include others in your pursuit. You are more likely to remain pure when you share the effort with others who have the same goal. Find, associate with, and be accountable to others who "call on the Lord from a pure heart" also.

Elevate the Word in Your Personal Life and in Your Ministry

I won't quote this lengthy passage, but I encourage you to read over it now—2 Timothy 3:10–4:4.

The basics don't change just because ministry is hard. Keep going back to the Word for your own personal encouragement. It is able to give you assurance and equip you to do the work of ministry.

This sounds a lot like points discussed earlier in this chapter. The emphasis Paul placed on the Word of God indicates how important it is! Keep preaching the Word. Do it when you feel like it and when you don't (2 Tim 4:2b). Preach in a way that challenges people where they live (v. 2c). Keep it up.

Encourage Someone Else Who Is Hurting

Take a minute and read 2 Timothy 4:9–22 as well.

Paul himself was going through a time of extreme hardship. He asked Timothy to "come to me soon" (v. 9) because others had abandoned him. As Paul speaks of being left to face the Roman trial by himself (v. 16), his personal hurt is evident—"all deserted me." But his letter is primarily focused on encouraging Timothy.

When we're discouraged, it can help us to spend time with hurting people in order to lift their spirits. It gets our focus off ourselves. It can break the downward spiral of self-pity and despondency. I don't know if this was part of Paul's reason for asking Timothy to come. He may have just wanted Timothy's company. But Paul evidently did not think that Timothy's discouraged state of mind would keep him from being an encouragement to Paul. And maybe Paul thought the trip would be good for Timothy. A visit to another discouraged Christian or hurting pastor might be just what *you* need!

Know That Whatever Happens, God Will Never Desert You

"He stands with you and strengthens you so the message will go out and the people who need it will hear" (my paraphrase of 2 Tim 4:17).

This is Paul's ultimate confidence for himself. He felt deserted and hurt (vv. 10, 14, 16). But He knew that the Lord had not abandoned him. These are beautiful words!

"But the Lord stood by me and strengthened me, so that through me the message might be fully proclaimed" (v. 17).

Paul took heart in the truth that His Savior was with Him when everyone else left him. I think he wanted his young friend Timothy to know that the Lord was with him during his painful season of ministry as well. These are good words for any hurting or discouraged pastor to read, cling to, and take to heart.

Paul, Timothy, and any discouraged minister of God can say, "The Lord will rescue me from every evil deed and bring me safely into his heavenly kingdom. To him be the glory forever and ever. Amen!" (v. 18).

TAKE ACTION

Rather than wallow in discouragement, identify three to five of these action steps you can implement in the next few months. Select one that is the most attainable or the most needed. Break it down into steps. Pray for wisdom and help from God. Start on it, and then another. Discouragement will come and go. You can faithfully carry out your work for the Lord regardless as you are enabled by His grace.

CHAPTER EIGHT

REFLECT AND DISCUSS

1. Are you discouraged, or could you potentially be, by something happening in your life or ministry right now? Identify your sources of discouragement so you can proactively address them.

2. Select action steps from 2 Timothy that best fit your discouragements. How can you start taking these actions? When can you put them into motion?

3. Are there ways you can bring encouragement to another man in ministry, such as a member of your pastoral team or another pastor you know? What actions can you take to encourage your brother pastors?

OVERPOWERING MINISTRY DISAPPOINTMENTS WITH KINGDOM HOPE

People will let you down. So will your church. God won't, but it can feel like He has. Disappointment can lead to disillusionment. You can lose your motivation to persevere and complete the ministry God has assigned to you.

Paul is an example to us in many ways, and one of them is dealing with disappointment. He experienced a severe degree of disappointment, but he was anchored to truth that gave him hope. Let's look at how this is described in 2 Timothy 4:9–18.

Very near the end of his life and ministry, the walls were closing in. He could see the forces moving into place that would bring about his demise. We can identify with some of the hard ministry realities Paul faced.

HARD MINISTRY REALITIES

Hurtful Desertion

We are familiar with these words in 2 Timothy 4:9–10 and the pain they represent—"Demas . . . has deserted me." There are about one hundred people named in Scripture associated with Paul in his ministry. About ten of them were "longtime coworkers." Demas may have been the last of these ten to associate himself with Paul.[1]

Paul mentioned Demas along with companions Luke and Mark in two other letters, calling him one of "my fellow workers" in Philemon 24. As a longtime coworker on Paul's ministry team, their relationship would have developed beyond a working one and become personal. The word "deserted" in 2 Timothy 4:10 is strong; it could be translated "abandoned." The reason was he was "in love with this present world." This is the opposite of how faithful servants are described in v. 8, as those "who have loved his appearing."[2]

Paul didn't say Demas had left the faith, but he definitely abandoned Paul. It might have been for his own safety that he didn't want to be associated with Paul, or for personal comfort, as Thessalonica may have been his home town ("gone to Thessalonica"). Though we don't fully understand his motivation, Demas was a deserter and Paul felt his abandonment very personally. He didn't hide his disappointment—"Timothy, come quickly, because Demas has left."

You likely have had people who profess to be Christians, attend your church, get involved in ministry, and work alongside you, then leave. You know you shouldn't take it personally, but you naturally do, because you are pouring your life into the church. You have developed a camaraderie in ministry, maybe even become close friends. You can't help feeling let down.

Another experience of this is when a family member turns away from God. You have an expectation that those who grow up in your home will follow the Lord. There is no greater joy than when your children walk in truth. When they do not, the depth of sorrow you feel can bring disillusionment with ministry and even with God.

---

1. Gerald F. Hawthorne, Ralph P. Martin, and Daniel G. Reid, *Dictionary of Paul and His Letters* (InterVarsity Press, 1993), 183.

2. Mounce, 589.

Circumstantial Separation

In 2 Timothy 4:10b–12 we see that some kind of ministry trips took "Crescens . . . to Galatia," "Titus to Dalmatia," and "Tychicus . . . to Ephesus." These people were colaborers with Paul. Ministry logistics moved them away. He longed for companionship—"Get Mark and bring him with you."

Ministry work can relocate people you care about away from you, or you away from them. Your youth pastor is called to be lead pastor at another church. A fellow elder or deacon has a job change and moves away. The local manufacturing plant closes, and church members have to relocate. Young people in your church grow up and move on to serve the Lord in another place. Your ministry assignment takes you away from family.

These are hard realities of ministry that may cause us to lose heart.

Material Deprivation

Paul not only felt the loss of companions, but experienced the hard reality of material deprivation (2 Tim 4:13). Paul requested his cloak, a blanket-like cape that would have kept him warm on cold nights in prison. "The books and . . . the parchments" were Paul's personal library, probably including Old Testament Scriptures, other writings, and his own notes for feeding his mind and spirit. He felt the lack of these important and comforting possessions. How would you feel if you couldn't get to your books?

Material possessions, especially when we are deprived of them, can be a source of disappointment. The parsonage needs repairs, and the church is slow to take care of them; your car keeps breaking down; there's no provision in the church budget for buying books, attending a conference, or working on a degree; you aren't provided with the time or resources for a real vacation, or even being able to eat out.

We can compare our situation with others in ministry or even church members who have more material provisions and opportunities and feel disappointment. Just like Paul felt the bite of cold that reminded him of what he didn't have, the pressures of life make us feel the lack of resources, and we can grow bitter toward the church or even God.

Malicious Opposition

Paul named another source of deep disappointment in 2 Timothy 4:14–15: "Alexander the coppersmith did me great harm." This is the hard reality of malicious opposition.

The word translated "did" means "demonstrated" or "showed." It was sometimes used of bringing legal charges. The term "much harm" (NKJV) is at the beginning of the sentence in Greek for emphasis. Literally it reads, "Much bad he showed to me."

Alexander may have reported Paul to the Roman authorities resulting in his current imprisonment. Verse 15 says "he strongly opposed our message," indicating he had turned Paul in or by some other act purposely attempted to sabotage the impact of the truth Paul was teaching and the gospel he was spreading.

You may have faced serious opposition to your ministry, even people in your church who seem to be working against you. God does not miss the wrong done to His cause or to His servant. It may seem like there are no consequences for these destructive people, but God will enact His justice in His way and time.

Notice how Paul handled this opposition. He prayed and trusted that God would carry out justice on Alexander: "the Lord will repay him according to his deeds" (v. 14). The future tense verb implies that even though there did not seem to be immediate consequences for this man's malicious acts, God would deal justly with him in His time.

Some situations we face will not be resolved until the Lord tests all of our works at the judgment seat of Christ. We need to commit the people and the hurt they cause to God. This doesn't mean we shouldn't address problems or confront those who cause them, especially if they are opposing the gospel or dividing God's people. But ultimately they will answer to God.

The hard realities of Paul's ministry and the accompanying disappointments piled up. But as is often the case, one hardship is overlapped by another.

Total Desolation

On top of all these circumstances, Paul faced the hard ministry reality of total desolation (2 Tim 4:16).

Paul faced a court hearing he called his "first defense." Imagine you've been arrested, locked in prison, separated from your family and friends, and deprived of material comforts, but you know people are praying for you. The initial hearing is scheduled, and you hope to catch a glimpse of someone you know who is there to support you, possibly even speak as a character witness on your behalf.

The sharp pain of betrayal by some will ease when loyal Christ-followers and true friends show up. As you're led into the courtroom for your arraignment, you realize the room is empty except for the judge, prosecutor, clerk, and guards. Your heart sinks. "No one came to stand by me, but all deserted me" (v. 16). You face one of the most difficult days of your life alone.

Understandably some may have kept their distance from the persecution in Rome, and others just weren't able to make it for various reasons. But imagine the thoughts that form in your mind and how you feel toward those people who could have been there but found someplace else to be. Your disappointment in that moment is palpable.

You may be in a similar place. It's the hardest time in your life and absolutely no one is showing up. You're totally alone. People you expect to encourage and help you aren't there. You feel abandoned.

We can learn from what Paul said next: "May it not be charged against them" (v. 16b). He was less concerned for himself and more concerned for them, for their relationship with God. He did not hold it against them, and if they sinned in some way, he wanted God to forgive them. His heart of forgiveness arose from genuine love for people that superseded self-preservation and protection.

It's natural to take it personally when people let you down. You might even wish bad things would happen to those who hurt you. You may feel satisfaction in their calamity. With God's grace you can love others and want the best for them. You can let go of the hurt and replace it with sincere desire for them to be right with God.

If Paul had hardened his heart and become bitter against his friends, he would have spiraled downward and lost the opportunity for God's glory to shine and the gospel to spread through him. But look at what he said next: "But the Lord stood by me and strengthened me, so that through me the message might be fully proclaimed and all the Gentiles might hear it" (v. 17). He made a choice to place his expectations, not on people or circumstances, but on truth.

Like Paul, you may be facing hard ministry realities. Like Paul, you can also focus on truth.

HOPEFUL KINGDOM TRUTHS

On one side of the balance, Paul had betrayal, abandonment, and isolation. He places on the other side, "But the Lord," referring to Jesus Christ (2 Tim 4:17).

This is the One who appeared on the road to Damascus to whom Paul cried, "Who are you Lord?" (Acts 9:5), the One whose commanding voice Paul heard that put him into the ministry. This is the same Lord who in Corinth spoke to Paul in the night by a vision, "'Do not be afraid, but go on speaking and do not be silent for I am with you, and no one will attack you to harm you, for I have many in this city who are my people.' And he stayed a year and six months, teaching the word of God among them" (Acts 18:9–11).

How much longer can *you* keep going, knowing the Lord is with you?

And just like on the storm-tossed ship, everyone had given up hope, and Paul announced to the despairing sailors and guards, "This very night there stood before me an angel of the God to whom I belong and whom I worship" (Acts 27:23). That angel assured him they would survive and he would see Rome.

This is the same Lord who was next to Paul at his court hearing when no one else was there! "The Lord stood by me" (2 Tim 4:17). Jesus fulfilled

His promise, once again, "I am with you always" (Matt 28:20); "I will never leave you nor forsake you" (Heb 13:5). The Lord did not disappoint Paul!

Conybeare and Howson's classic volume describes Paul's situation so eloquently: "No advocate pled his cause, no attorney aided him in arranging the evidence, no patron appeared in his support, no friends showed to plead for lenience, as was the custom in the courts of Rome. But he had a more powerful intercessor, and a wiser advocate, who could never leave him or forsake him. The Lord Jesus was always near him, but now was felt almost visibly present in the hour of his need. . . . His earthly friends deserted him but his heavenly friend stood by him."[3]

Your Lord's empowering presence enables you to finish what God assigned you to do.

In conjunction with Jesus Christ's nearness, signified by "and" in 2 Timothy 4:17, is His strength. He "strengthened me" could be translated "empowered." A. T. Robertson translates it "He poured power into me."[4]

Here's the promise: you can be empowered by Jesus Christ. He will pour His power into you to meet whatever hardships you face and the disappointments they bring. During times of material need, you can say, like Paul, "I can do all things through him who strengthens me" (Phil 4:13). Like the younger man in ministry challenged by Paul, you can "be strengthened by the grace that is in Christ Jesus" (2 Tim 2:1). Strength from Christ is needed by and available for the Timothys and the Pauls.

Empowered for what? "So that through me the message might be fully proclaimed" (2 Tim 4:17). God strengthened Paul so that he could fulfill his mission and complete the assignment given to him by God.

Just as God gave Paul an assignment, He has given you one as well. Have you completed it? If not, there is strength from God in equal measure to all

---

3. W. J. Conybeare and J. S. Howson, *The Life and Epistles of St. Paul* (Wm. B. Eerdmans, reprinted 1983), 768–9.

4. A. T. Robertson, *Word Pictures in the New Testament, The Epistles of Paul*, (Baker Book House, 1931), 4:633.

the responsibilities, the burdens, and the problems that go with finishing what He sent you there to do.

Your Lord's sovereign protection keeps you going as long as God intends you to serve.

Paul added another comment about a past experience—"So I was rescued from the lion's mouth" (v. 17). Ideas of what Paul was referring to include Nero, a previous imprisonment with a potential death sentence, or Satan. This figure of speech signifies that he was snatched from the jaws of death.

Who or what is your *lion*? Is there someone who is adversarial, even aggressive, a threat to you, your family, or ministry?

My wife and I were tubing with friends on the Root River in Minnesota. As we came to a bend in the river, the current took us toward the outside bank into the roots of a fallen tree. Rafters and kayakers know the danger of these hazards called "strainers" that can force you underwater and trap you there.

When Faith's tube hit the roots, the front flipped up, spilling her into the water. The current pinned her against the roots. Just her head remained above the water, her legs pushed forward under the roots, unable to move because of the force of the current. I was still on my tube, hanging on to the roots with one hand and her with the other. With the relentless current she couldn't move, and I couldn't get her loose. She was in immediate danger of being pushed under by the current and trapped in the tangle of roots. In that moment I knew I could lose her, and our day of fun would come to a tragic end.

She was holding on to a root to keep her head above water, and I don't know why, but I said, "Let go." She did, and the current spun her away from the roots, took her under, where she bounced along the rocky bottom, then popped out downstream. She was bruised and shaken, and after we recovered her tube, I held her hand tight almost the rest of the trip downriver. I've never been so conscious of the possibility of death and of God's hand of protection.

Our experience captures the idea of Paul's experience as well. "Rescued" in verse 17 means to be snatched from danger. The unseen hand in Paul's case was of course the Lord. Whether you face a threat to life or ministry, God will keep you safe and pull you through for as long as He has plans for you in His work.

Paul then looked forward and upward, beyond present circumstances. "The Lord will rescue me from every evil deed and bring me safely into his heavenly kingdom" (v. 18). "The Lord" is the same Jesus. "Will" represents the same confidence. "Rescue" is the same kind of deliverance. "Bring me safely" is talking about the final stage of salvation—going to be with the Lord! "From every evil deed" is the evil done against him. Paul was saved from *his* sins, but also from the sins *others* committed against him, such as Demas, Alexander, and the government of Rome. He would be saved from the penalty, the power, the presence, and all the problems of sin!

We are not only saved from but also saved to—what?—"his heavenly kingdom" (v. 18). Literally this says, "Unto the kingdom of him, the heavenly." It's not talking about a kingdom here and now, but future and eternal, under the fully realized reign of the King of kings and Lord of lords.

This leads to one more hopeful kingdom truth.

Your Lord's ultimate deliverance guarantees you safe passage to His heavenly kingdom in eternal glory.

Read this slowly and consider what awaits you. "And there shall be no more curse, but the throne of God and of the Lamb shall be in it, and His servants shall serve Him. They shall see His face, and His name shall be on their foreheads. There shall be no night there: They need no lamp nor light of the sun, for the Lord God gives them light. And they shall reign forever and ever" (Rev 22:3–5 NKJV).

FOLLOWING FOOTPRINTS

As we trace the final steps of Paul's life, if we look closely, we can see that he was walking in the footprints of another who had gone this way before him.

Betrayed by a close companion. Tried by the Roman government. Deserted by his friends. Forsaken in his most trying hour. His words—"The Lord will repay" (2 Tim 4:14).

Peter tells us our Savior, while on the cross, was "entrusting himself to him who judges righteously" (1 Pet 2:23). And Paul's words in 2 Timothy 4:16, "May it not be charged against them," sound a lot like, "Father, forgive them; for they do not know what they are doing" (Luke 23:34 NASB).

Paul portrays for us a Christlike response to deep disappointment. In the same way your disappointments are opportunities to grow a Christlike heart and to show a Christlike response. When you suffer in ministry, you follow in the footsteps of Christ. This is Christ in you, the hope of glory. Growing daily like Christ and being forever with Christ is our kingdom hope!

So finish your fight. Complete your course. Keep the faith. You have God's empowering presence with you. You have His sovereign protection over you. Christ likeness is being shaped in you. And ultimate, eternal deliverance is ahead of you.

REFLECT AND DISCUSS

1. Can you identify with any of the hard realities that caused Paul disappointment? Which ones? Are you going through other hard personal or ministry experiences that may lead to disillusionment with people, ministry, or even God?

2. Select one or more kingdom truths presented in this chapter that especially help you deal with disappointment in ministry. Take a few minutes and meditate on them, praying for God to help you anchor your thoughts, emotions, and decisions to these truths.

3. What are some ways you can develop a Christlike heart and response to people and circumstances in ministry that let you down?

CHAPTER TEN

THE ANTIDOTE FOR COMPARISON

COMPARISON TENDENCIES

Comparison eats at pastors. We tend to measure other pastors, categorize them in our minds, and rank ourselves accordingly. This leads to viewing those men and their ministries through a lens of either condescension or envy.

Peter had a problem with comparison. When Jesus predicted the disciples would abandon Him at His arrest, Peter claimed, "Though they all fall away because of you, I will never fall away" (Matt 26:33). Peter believed himself to be a better man than James, Matthew, Andrew, John, Thomas, and the rest of the twelve. We know how that turned out.

This comparison reflex did not go away when Peter reconciled with Jesus and was commissioned to spiritual leadership. We know this because, as usual, whatever was on Peter's mind came out of his mouth. The exchange between Jesus and Peter is recorded in John 21.

After reestablishing fellowship with Peter—"Do you love me?" "Yes, I love you."—Jesus oriented him toward his new calling: "Feed my sheep" (vv. 15–17). Peter's shepherding vocation would take him down a hard path to a painful end: "'Truly, truly, I say to you, when you were young, you used to dress yourself and walk wherever you wanted, but when you are old, you will stretch out your hands, and another will dress you and carry you where you do not want to go.' (This He said to show by what death He was to glorify God.) And after saying this He said to him, 'Follow me'" (John 21:18–19). Although Peter may not have fully understood it then, Jesus was predicting Peter's ministry would lead to imprisonment and an agonizing death.

As they walked and talked, John lingered close by. He enjoyed a unique closeness to Jesus. As John recounted this event, he called himself "the disciple whom Jesus loved, the one who also had leaned back against Him during the supper and had said, 'Lord, who is it that is going to betray you?'" (John 21:20). John enjoyed the privilege of being positioned in the number one spot near Jesus during the Last Supper and sharing very personal conversation with Him.

I wonder if the details of John's proximity to Jesus are included in this narrative to highlight John's intimacy in contrast to Judas's betrayal and Peter's denial. For some reason, Peter compared himself to John. Whether he was thinking of John's privileged relationship, or just because he was in view, Peter blurted, "Lord, what about this man?" (John 21:21).

COMPARISON TRAPS

We all have our comparison traps. Other churches in your community have full parking lots and hold multiple weekend services, while your membership has plateaued or is declining. Your friend from seminary days gets invited to speak at national conferences, and your only outside speaking engagement is the local Rotary club luncheon. As you hear a bivocational pastor describe the struggle of meeting the demands of a full-time job, church responsibilities, and a growing family, you feel pity from the vantage point of your fully paid pastoral position with support staff. Or you feel envy if the circumstances are reversed. You visit a church while on vacation and have a running critique going through your head of the facilities, the volunteers, and the sermon, affirming yourself for how you do it better or wishing you could.

The possibilities are endless as our naturally prideful hearts evaluate, calculate, categorize, and pass judgment on others or ourselves. We feel the Holy Spirit's conviction in our hearts about it. How can we put off this unholy attitude?

CHRIST-FOCUSED TRUTHS

Attack the comparison mentality with the truth Jesus spoke to Peter. He said, "If it is my will that he remain until I come, what is that to you? You follow me!" (John 21:22). Jesus wasn't stating that John wouldn't die (see v. 23). He was making a point.

Jesus said to Peter in essence, "If God in His sovereign plan determines John will be exempt from the natural laws of aging and death, or maybe walk with God and disappear into heaven like Enoch, or that a fiery chariot will pick him up and drop him off in glory like Elijah, but you, before you've even finished out your natural time on earth, will be tortured and executed as a criminal, dying in the worst, most shameful way, the difference is not your concern. You have no right to expect the same treatment as the other guy. Your circumstances may seem inequitably harsh. But I am the Chief Shepherd. Keep your eyes on me. Complete my will for you. You, Peter, you follow me."

Your ministry setting, the people you shepherd, and the circumstances in each season of your ministry are all part of the Chief Shepherd's assignment for you. Stop comparing yourself with others. You, pastor friend, you keep your eyes on Jesus. You follow Christ.

Notice Jesus's words, "If it is my will . . . you follow me" (v. 22). Literally the first part says, "If I am willing him." Several translations say, "If I want him" (NASB, NET, CSB, NIV). Young's Literal Translation captures the essence—"If him I will to remain till I come, what—to thee?"

Jesus claimed absolute authority over the circumstances of John's life, even how long John lived, and by implication, over the circumstances and longevity of Peter's life, and the manner of his death as well (vv. 18–19).

Jesus revealed that He has a specific will for individuals and their ministries. He had a sovereignly determined plan for John and a different one for Peter. This reality applies to us. Jesus Christ sovereignly determines the circumstances of a pastor's life and ministry. Peter himself later articulated the truth that each pastor's flock consists of "those allotted to your charge" (1 Pet 5:3 NKJV). Christ's will may include what we view as favorable circumstances or unfavorable circumstances. And His will for one pastor and ministry may vary significantly from another's. The myriad differences among local church ministries reflect Christ's multifaceted design for His church-building work.

How can you gain control of your comparison reflex? Start with submitting yourself to the sovereign will of the Chief Shepherd, Jesus Christ. Turn Jesus's words into a daily prayer: "Lord Jesus, I bow to you and submit to your will for me and my ministry. Help me not to concern myself with the seeming advantages or disadvantages of others. Jesus, I'm following you."

Then you can rejoice with and pray for others with a sincere heart. "Lord, thank you for how you are blessing my brother and his ministry. Give him wisdom to shepherd his flock through this season of prosperity. Guide him in using his gifts to minister for your glory. Keep Satan from gaining an advantage and tearing down what you are building up." Or, "Lord, I see my brother struggling under heavy burdens. Channel grace to him for every difficult situation he faces. Strengthen him to fulfill your will for his ministry. Help him to follow you."

Turn the comparison impulse into a reminder that Jesus Christ is preeminent in the church; it is His right to assign undershepherds where He wills, and each of us is responsible to follow Him.

CHAPTER TEN

REFLECT AND DISCUSS

1. What are your comparison traps? What do you tend to evaluate about yourself or your ministry and either envy or pity others depending on how they differ from you?

2. Take a few minutes to articulate a prayer responding to Jesus's charge, "*What is that to you? You follow me.*"

3. Formulate and express prayers of thanks and intercession for those to whom you compare yourself.

UNDERSTANDING COMPASSION FATIGUE

"THAT'S COMPASSION FATIGUE"

I was describing the emotional toll that ministry takes on pastors while they are encouraging and counseling people who experience especially difficult times. The person I was speaking to had received training for this very thing as an emergency medical technician. He said, "That's compassion fatigue."

I had never heard the term and was not familiar with the concept. When he explained it, lights came on. People in helping professions, including medical personnel, social workers, and clergy, are repeatedly exposed to deep and complicated problems in the course of their work. They can develop a mindset of detachment that reflects diminished compassion for the person they are helping. When I heard this description, I recognized it in my own experience.

I also recognized another phenomenon he described to me—vicarious trauma or secondary trauma. This occurs when a helper walks through a traumatic experience with someone, such as a church member or counselee, and bears much of the impact that comes with that traumatic scenario. For example, a man's wife leaves him for another man or another woman.

Or a young couple is killed in a tragic accident, leaving an orphaned child. Or a woman addicted to drugs is destroying her family.

The pastor pours time and energy—physical, emotional, and spiritual—into these situations. These life-altering, cataclysmic scenarios are on his mind day and night and are the subject of many conversations with his spouse. Bearing this weight takes a toll. The secondary trauma puts a strain on him and can lead to compassion fatigue.

The primary problem with compassion fatigue is losing the ability to care. Pastoral care is not only a set of practices. It requires an attitude of genuine care for individuals. We are commanded to love others. This means we are genuinely concerned for their well-being. Compassion is the ability to feel with someone who is hurting. If we become desensitized to the point of detachment, the element of love is removed. We are in danger of performing pastoral work in a clinical, professional, or mechanical manner.

A secondary effect of compassion fatigue is we feel guilty about it, which can turn into a downward spiral of discouragement. A pastor one day realizes he has lost his capacity to feel people's burdens with them. As a church member shares a concern, the pastor wishes he could be somewhere else. He drags himself to another visit. He dreads the next counseling appointment. He can't bring himself to write down church members' prayer requests and intercede for them at the throne of grace.

He knows he should be compelled by love and find joy in serving others. He feels guilty for his reluctance and becomes discouraged about ministry when he feels the urge to run away from hurting people rather than move toward them.

ORIGIN AND DEFINITION OF THE TERM

Dr. Charles Figley[1] defines compassion fatigue as "a state of tension

1. Dr. Charles Figley is the Tulane University Distinguished Chair in Disaster Mental Health and Associate Dean for Research and Director of the Traumatology Institute. He authored *Compassion Fatigue: Coping with Secondary Traumatic Stress Disorder in Those Who Treat the Traumatized*. Figley has published numer-

and preoccupation with the traumatized patients by re-experiencing the traumatic events. . . . It is a function of being witness to the suffering of others."[2]

The term "compassion fatigue" was first used in a study of burnout in nurses conducted in 1992. Pastors will readily recognize the similarities between nurses' experience and theirs. A description of this study states, "Multiple environmental stressors, such as expanding workload and long hours, coupled with the need to respond to complex patient needs, including pain, traumatic injury, and emotional distress, resulted in nurses feeling tired, depressed, angry, ineffective, apathetic, and detached." The description goes on to say,

> Nurses are particularly vulnerable to compassion fatigue. They often enter the lives of others at very critical junctures and become partners, rather than observers, in patients' healthcare journeys. Acute care nurses in particular often develop empathic engagement with patients and families. This, coupled with their experience of cumulative grief, positions them at the epicenter of an environment often characterized by sadness and loss. Nurses are frequently enmeshed in existential issues surrounding life and death.[3]

How does this phenomenon among nurses relate to pastors? Three faculty members of the University of Ulster in Northern Ireland published a study on compassion fatigue among clergy. Elements of the study address the impact on clergy of ministering to people affected by the 9/11

---

ous additional articles and anthology chapters on this and related subjects.

2. Charles Figley, "Compassion Fatigue. Psychotherapists' Chronic Lack of Self Care," *Journal of Clinical Practice*, session 58: 1435.

3. Deborah A. Boyle, "Countering Compassion Fatigue: A Requisite Nursing Agenda," *The Online Journal of Issues in Nursing*, 16(01), https://ojin.nursing-world.org/table-of-contents/volume-16-2011/number-1-january-2011/counter-ing-compassion-fatigue/.

terrorist attacks. The effect included "significant levels of compassion fatigue." They warned, "There is a price being paid as a result of vicarious involvement within the course of the daily pastoral ministry that entails seemingly less major events . . . but which involves daily exposure to the pain of others."[4]

Pastors experience mini-9/11s on a regular basis. The call that sends you to the emergency room to comfort a family in shock, the family breakup, runaway teenager, adultery exposed—you carry the pain of others in your heart and feel the anguish in a similar way as they do. And this is multiplied times the number of people you have in your church.

The Chicago-based Biblical Counseling Center says on this topic, "In clinical settings, compassion fatigue is sometimes referred to as 'secondary trauma' or 'vicarious traumatization.' It may also be considered similar to a type of PTSD[5] that affects those who provide soul care to trauma victims."[6]

The American Institute of Stress defines compassion fatigue as "the emotional residue or strain of exposure to working with those suffering from the consequences of traumatic events."[7] One Christian counselor says, "Generally, it is caused when one has become so involved in providing care to others that they become emotionally and spiritually exhausted"[8] Compassion fatigue is sometimes described as the cost of caring.

---

4. Jill Anne Hendron, Pauline Irving, and Brian J. Taylor, "Clergy Stress through Working with Trauma: a Qualitative Study of Secondary Impact," *Journal of Pastoral Care and Counseling*, 68(4), https://doi.org/10.1177/154230501406800404.

5. PTSD is post-traumatic stress disorder, a mental health condition associated with traumatic events, whether experienced first-hand or witnessed.

6. "Help for Compassion Fatigue," https://biblicalcounselingcenter.org/help-compassion-fatigue/.

7. "What Is Compassion Fatigue?" https://www.cheservices.com/blog/what-is-compassion-fatigue.

8. Terri Lackey, "Compassion Fatigue Is Sign of Caregiver Burnout, Self Says," Baptist Press, May 5, 2002. https://www.baptistpress.com/resource-library/news/compassion-fatigue-is-sign-of-caregiver-burnout-self-says/.

MANIFESTATIONS OF COMPASSION FATIGUE

There are numerous lists. Some symptoms sound like normal human struggles, or even fleshly responses to difficult people and situations. However, if these are a pattern, especially several of them together, and they become more pronounced over a period of time, possibly in a way that is noticed by people who know you, you may want to consider that compassion fatigue is a factor. I've selected some of the more prominent, noticeable symptoms:

- **Physical**—fatigue, lack of endurance, loss of strength, difficulty sleeping, somatic problems (headaches, colds, ulcers)

- **Emotional**—irritability, anger, anxiety, depression, apathy, cynicism, becoming jaded, hardened to people and their problems, discouragement, feeling overwhelmed, attitude of hopelessness

- **Behavioral**—aggression, callousness, pessimism, defensiveness, loss of interest in behaviors once enjoyed, withdrawal from family or friends

- **Spiritual**—decrease in discernment, disinterest in introspection, lack of spiritual awareness, poor judgment

- **Intellectual**—boredom, disorderliness, weakened attention to detail

- **Work-Related**—absenteeism, tardiness, avoidance of intense patient situations, impersonal communication[9]

The bottom line is, "You can't hear other people's pain without being affected by it. If you aren't affected, that's a true sign of compassion fatigue."[10]

---

9. Boyle, Lackey.

10. Lackey.

SCRIPTURAL SOLUTIONS FOR COMPASSION FATIGUE

A pastor can proactively mitigate compassion fatigue, or experience recovery and renewal if needed, by meditating on these biblical realities.

We are all called to bear one another's burdens.

Galatians 6:2 says, "Bear one another's burdens, and so fulfill the law of Christ." This is a normal part of Christian fellowship and ministry. So we should not withdraw ourselves from helping others through their trials and tragedies.

There is a cost of ministering to others.

Paul wrote, "So, being affectionately desirous of you, we were ready to share with you not only the gospel of God but also our own selves, because you had become very dear to us" (1 Thess 2:8). And to the Corinthians, "And I will very gladly spend and be spent for your souls; though the more abundantly I love you, the less I am loved" (2 Cor 12:15, NKJV). Jesus "came not to be served but to serve, and to give his life as a ransom for many" (Mark 10:45). He is our model for servant leadership, and it cost Him His life. So we need to count the cost and be willing to pay a price.

God can strengthen us for the rigors of ministry work.

Paul encouraged Timothy, "You therefore, my son, be strong in the grace that is in Christ Jesus" (2 Tim 2:1, NKJV). Paul himself labored to exhaustion, but received strength from God: "Him we proclaim, warning everyone and teaching everyone with all wisdom, that we may present everyone mature in Christ. For this I toil, struggling with all his energy that he powerfully works within me" (Col 1:28–29).

We need to regularly receive strength from the Lord through prayer, nourishment from the Word of God, and Christian fellowship. If we let these go, we will be quickly depleted and overwhelmed by the burden of caring for the souls of others.

Remember we are finite beings with human limitations.

Although God empowers us for ministry work that exceeds our natural ability to perform, He does not eliminate the need for normal human sustenance such as food and rest. And we can reach our capacity for handling major, traumatic scenarios. There is a point where we reach overload. It's okay to say, "I need help with this."

Rest in God's omniscient, omnipotent, omnipresent involvement in people's traumatic life events.

God is present and active in people's lives all the time. I can do my best to deal with a hard situation, then go to bed at night and know that, although I'm not with that person, God is and He is at work—comforting, providing, sanctifying.

Trust in the process of inner progressive sanctification through the Word and the Holy Spirit.

Part of the problem is thinking I am the Savior, the one with ability to do all the things. If someone is going to change, recover, or gain hope, I believe I am going to produce it or at least be the key to facilitating it. It comes down to our view of God, His sovereignty, and progressive sanctification.

> The foundation of prevention and healing is trust and rest in the work of Christ. . . . The hope that counselors extend to counselees is the same hope upon which their faith rests, namely, the gospel of Jesus Christ. . . . only God is infinite. Only He, working in and through the power of His word and Spirit, is able to accomplish the goal of biblical soul care: sanctification.[11]

---

11. Joshua Waulk, "Too Tired to Care," Biblicalcounselingcoalition.org, June 29, 2016. https://www.biblicalcounselingcoalition.org/2016/06/29/too-tired-to-care/.

PRACTICAL SOLUTIONS

In addition to appropriating scriptural truths, there are practical ways to overcome compassion fatigue in ministry.

Manage your weekly schedule.

Establish priorities and commit time to them. Build in "sabbath rest"—a rhythm of life that includes not only sufficient sleep but also regular breaks from ministry work.

Block out times when you do not counsel.

Avoid counseling on your day off, heavy sermon preparation days, and weekends, except for emergencies.

Determine a realistic load of pastoral care for your role and enlist others to share the work.

Utilize your pastoral team, elders, retired pastors, deacons, or a biblical counseling center.

Have someone you can talk to.

Find someone to help you carry your burden (see Gal 6:2). Proactively involve someone else. Pastors naturally share a lot with their spouses, but it's healthy to have another colleague or confidante with whom to share ministry burdens.

Steward your personal life and priorities for long-term ministry.

This includes sufficient rest, healthful diet, regular exercise, consistent and meaningful personal devotion, spiritual growth, appropriate commitments of time, energy, and attention to marriage, family, ministry, and friendships, along with discernment in saying yes or no when necessary. These are all addressed in this book as critical to a pastor's overall well-being.

Practice an unhurried pace of grace like Jesus.

Consider this approach to ministry that is recommended in the *Journal of Christian Nursing* addressing the issue of compassion fatigue:

> Jesus followed the pace God set for him, rather than what people expected of him. He didn't send away the Canaanite woman asking for help (Matt 15:21–28); didn't rush to heal Lazarus (John 11:6); and he stopped to help a sick woman when a centurion's daughter was dying (Mark 5:22–34). Yet at the end of his life, he had completed everything God had given him to do (John 17:4, 19:30).

> Fadling[12] calls this the 'pace of grace' (p. 10), an unhurried, relaxed way of the heart that accepts what God thinks of us and follows Jesus's lead. This pace of grace lets God guide what I should and should not be doing: to work or to rest. Fadling (says),

> "Just as surely as God gives us ministry opportunities, he also gives us opportunities to rest with him and be restored."[13]

So let us learn to work when it's time to work, rest when it's time to rest, bear what we are meant to bear of our own and others' burdens, and trust our all-powerful God, our ever-present Savior, and our continually-working Paraclete, the Holy Spirit, to accomplish the real work of comfort, restoration, and spiritual progress in people's lives.

---

12. The author is quoting from *An Unhurried Life: Following Jesus' Rhythms of Work and Rest* by Alan Fadling.

13. Kathy Schoonover-Shoffner, "Hidden Component of Compassion Fatigue?" *Journal of Christian Nursing*, 32(2): 70, April/June 2015, https://journals.lww.com/journalofchristiannursing/fulltext/2015/04000/hidden_component_of_compassion_fatigue_.1.aspx.

CHAPTER ELEVEN

REFLECT AND DISCUSS

1. Do you recognize any indications that you may be experiencing compassion fatigue? What are they?

2. Which of the scriptural solutions is most helpful for you? How can you embed these in your thoughts about ministry work?

3. Which of the practical solutions is most helpful for you? How can you implement these into your routine?

PART 4

ESSENTIAL PRACTICES

COMMUNION WITH GOD

THE CORE OF PASTORAL HEALTH

It's a sad reality that pastors can have an anemic devotional life. Nothing is more important in the life of a minister of the Word of God than personal fellowship with the God of the Word. If a pastor's personal relationship with God suffers, everything else is in jeopardy.

Communion with God is at the core of pastoral health. By communion I mean personal, meaningful interaction between God and you. And by interaction, I mean God speaking to you through His Word and you speaking to God through prayer.

Research confirms the critical role communion with God has in pastoral health. As cited in chapter 1, the authors of *Faithful and Fractured: Responding to the Clergy Health Crisis* report, "The vast majority of pastors with flourishing mental health, compared to only about half of those with burnout, expressed intentionality in personal care . . . [which] included things like . . . spiritual practices (like prayer or Bible reading)."[1]

I've started making a distinction in my mind between *devotions* and *devotion*. "Doing devotions," or "devos" is common Christian-speak, but this terminology feels to me like fulfilling an obligation or completing a task.

I'm helped by thinking of this practice as spending time in devotion. *Devotions* is an act while *devotion* is an attitude of the heart. Pastor, do you

---

1. Proeschold-Bell and Byassee, 139.

commune with your heavenly Father? Do you spend time in devotion to your Savior?

One enemy of this all-important pursuit is the urge to view the Bible primarily as source material for sermons rather than God's own message to you. Some of us find it difficult to read a passage of Scripture without outlining it for preaching. Another barrier to meaningful devotion is familiarity with the Bible. You've studied it for years, maybe decades, and it feels stale when you turn to the next passage on your reading schedule. Nothing is new.

Regarding prayer, distractions are always present for any Christian. But it seems as pastors we are prone to allowing the name or face of someone we're praying for to take us down a rabbit hole of rehearsing difficult situations involving that person, whether real or imaginary. Prayer compounds our stress rather than mitigating it.

There are numerous helpful resources providing motivation and practical help with spiritual disciplines, so I won't duplicate those here. But I do want to make a few suggestions and share some personal examples to encourage your personal communion with God.

Meaningful and Fresh

How can you overcome staleness in your devotional life? Some do just fine with a typical reading schedule, such as going through the Bible annually, combined with a routine prayer time. I find my attention wandering or I feel like I'm rushing through chapters just to stay on schedule.

Using a variety of approaches to reading God's Word helps keep it fresh for me. Right now I'm reading slowly through the historical books of the Old Testament and outlining them in a journal along with truths that stand out to me. I'll read through a major section, then go back and read it again, then outline it. As devotional thoughts or applications come to mind, I enter them in my journal.

I've also read one book of the Bible repeatedly for a month, keeping a journal of observations, truths, and applications that stand out to me. By the time I'm finished, I've spent significant time in that portion of

God's Word and noticed details that hadn't caught my attention before. The practice of journaling fulfills my pastoral instinct to capture important thoughts in writing but keeps it on a personal level. Of course, I may go back later and draw sermon material from what I've recorded—what could be better than preaching truth that I've already processed through my own heart and life!

Another more laborious but rewarding method of Scripture intake is to translate it out of the original language. My wife gave me a set of Greek Scripture Journals[2] as a very nice birthday gift, and I love them. I can make my own translation between the lines and note textual observations and devotional thoughts in the spacious margins. Translating rather than just reading forces me to focus on individual words, grammatical features, and other details instead of skimming over them. The labor of translation becomes personal engagement with the Word for me rather than just a step in the process of sermon preparation.

I keep a prayer journal where I write Scripture that encourages and guides me as I pray along with lists of people and requests I'm regularly bringing to God. I like to read through the verses and let them help me form my thoughts as I praise, give thanks, and ask.

Some of my most meaningful times of pure communion with God in prayer happen on outdoor walks. Getting out of the house lessens distractions. The light activity of walking is invigorating, when I might be dozing off while praying in a chair or kneeling by a couch. Nature prompts praise to the Creator. My heart flows freely through what I know to be true about my God, people I'm burdened for, and the joys and challenges of my own life, and I pour these out to God as I walk.

Now let me give you something to think about. Recently my wife and I were challenged about the idea of fasting and praying. I know there are different views on whether fasting is a necessary practice in our day. I'm not going to argue for it here. But experientially it has intensified our prayers in a new way. The pastors in the network that planted our church practice

---

2. *Greek Scripture Journal: New Testament Set,* 19 volumes (Crossway, 2020).

this weekly. When our pastor mentioned it, we decided to implement it into our spiritual walk.

We usually fast one day a week from after dinner one night to dinner the next night. I eat half of an energy bar with my coffee first thing in the morning so I don't get jittery. Since I'm doing my regular work through the day, I may have a small snack of crackers or nuts in the mid- or late afternoon to maintain stamina. During the times I would normally eat a meal, I meditate on Scripture and spend time in prayer.

I've found this weekly rhythm of light fasting raises my spiritual focus and pushes me to pray more specifically, passionately, and dependently. It definitely refreshes my routine efforts and elevates prayer to a place of importance that positively affects my prayer times on other days as well.

Consistent but Flexible

I've been asked what a normal week is like for a pastor. That usually prompts a laugh. You know what I mean. The unpredictability of ministry work can easily throw you off the important routines you need to maintain, including your devotional life.

Nighttime ministry work might bump you off schedule, especially if morning is your normal time for devotion. Since the average church member's daytime hours are occupied with work and other commitments, evenings are the best time for visits, meetings, and counseling appointments. Emergency calls can keep you out in the wee hours. Dragging yourself out of bed early enough to spend time with God before entering your day can be painful.

I suggest allowing yourself flexibility with your office start time. If you're normally in your office or study at 8:00 a.m., don't feel bad about showing up at 9:00. This might warrant a conversation with your fellow elders or possibly your deacons, explaining how a pastor's schedule works.

In fact I've seen a pastor's schedule model that divides the day into thirds—morning, afternoon, and evening. A normal work day covers two of the three parts of the day. So if a pastor is going to be out all evening, he is free to spend either that morning or afternoon off duty.[3]

Ultimately, don't bind your conscience to a standard that God doesn't require. I know there are many good arguments for daily personal time in the Word and prayer. But missing a day doesn't knock you out of favor with God. You may feel spiritually weak, like you've missed a meal, but the Spirit is still in you, and the throne of grace is still open to you. Walk dependently through that day in prayer, find a few minutes to meditate on a short portion of Scripture, and look forward to the next opportunity to enjoy extended communion with your Savior again.

Positive as Well as Preventative

Communion with God has positive benefits, but also provides preventative effects. One I'd like to address is in the area of temptation.

Pastor, what are your temptations? No doubt you've tried to eliminate them from your life but have found that an impossible endeavor. You've probably counseled others this way; now let me counsel you. Develop a personal walk with God that generates deep love for Him. When temptation comes, your love for your Savior will enable, even compel you to resist its power over you.

Take a look at 1 John 2:15–17. I think "of the Father" in verse 15 is an objective genitive. So the instruction, "Do not love the world or the things in the world. If anyone loves the world, the **love of the Father** is not in him" is saying that our affections and passions are either directed toward the world or toward God.

Verse 16 identifies the channels through which we can be tempted as "the desires of the flesh and the desires of the eyes and pride of life." This means we naturally love pleasure, material things, physical experiences, and ourselves. Your besetting temptations arouse your desires in these areas. If you habitually give in to them, you do not love God. That's strong, but that's what this text is saying.

---

3. John Piper, "How Can Pastors Guard Their Time with Their Families?" DesiringGod.org, https://www.desiringgod.org/interviews/how-can-pastors-guard-their-time-with-their-families.

On the other hand, if you love God, you will be much less likely to give in to your temptations. As John says later in his letter, "For this is the love of God, that we keep his commandments" (1 John 5:3). Loving God compels you to do His will. How do you grow in your love for God? By knowing Him, as John said: "Anyone who does not love does not know God, because God is love" (1 John 4:8). He's primarily addressing our love for others, but I think we can infer that knowing God will result in loving Him as well.

What does this have to do with your personal communion with God? If you are truly having times of devotion, not just doing devotions, then your intimate knowledge of God will deepen, resulting in your love for God becoming more abiding, invigorating, and compelling. Of course you will still need to avoid situations where temptation lurks, discipline yourself to deny appetites and passions, and practice transparency with brothers in Christ who have your back.

But you will enjoy sweet days when you pillow your head with the realization your besetting temptation remained merely a shadow in the edges of your day rather than eclipsing your joy in God. You will give thanks that the love of your heart and the passion of your life that day was directed toward the One who loved you and gave Himself for you.

LEADERS NEED GOD'S WORD

I'd like to end this chapter by encouraging you with a text of Scripture that emphasizes the importance of a leader's personal engagement with the Word of God. Deuteronomy 17 includes a record of God's instructions to the Israelites concerning their king. In addition to the requirement of being an Israelite (vv. 14–15), there is a precautionary instruction concerning his heart in verses 16–17: "Only he must not acquire many horses for himself or cause the people to return to Egypt in order to acquire many horses, since the Lord has said to you, 'You shall never return that way again.' And he shall not acquire many wives for himself, lest his heart turn away, nor shall he acquire for himself excessive silver and gold."

The king should not own an excessive number of horses, he should not have multiple wives, and he should not accumulate large amounts of gold. These were symbols of political power, material wealth, and sensual indulgence. The kings were to guard against the downfalls of many leaders—pride, sensuality, and materialism.

God also gave specific instructions for a very important practice that was to be part of every king's daily schedule—reading the Scriptures.

> And when he sits on the throne of his kingdom, he shall write for himself in a book a copy of this law, approved by the Levitical priests. And it shall be with him, and he shall read in it all the days of his life, that he may learn to fear the Lord his God by keeping all the words of this law and these statutes, and doing them, that his heart may not be lifted up above his brothers, and that he may not turn aside from the commandment, either to the right hand or to the left, so that he may continue long in his kingdom, he and his children, in Israel. (Deut 17:18–20)

The kings were instructed to not only read the Scriptures consistently ("all the days of his life") but also purposefully ("that" followed by several specific purposes.)

You and I are not kings in Israel, but this is still an example for us. God places a high priority on consistent, frequent intake of the Word of God for those who serve Him. And we, too, are susceptible to becoming inflated with pride, captivated by materialism, and indulging our flesh in sinful, sensual pleasures. We need a resource that guides us to live in a way that pleases God and helps us grow in our character and behavior so we reflect His priorities in our lives. Just like the Scriptures were the means for doing all of this for the kings of Israel, they are for us today as well.

Read the Bible to know God—"that he may learn to fear the Lord his God"; to know what to do in daily life and ministry—"by keeping all the words of this law and these statutes, and doing them"; to help you stay humble—"that his heart may not be lifted up above his brothers";

to prevent personal failure—"that he may not turn aside from the commandment, either to the right hand or to the left"; and for longevity in ministry—"so that he may continue long in his kingdom, he and his children, in Israel."

Think of the first three kings of Israel! Saul became arrogantly self-willed. David fell to adultery. Solomon became enamored of wealth and pleasure. I wonder if these leaders allowed their daily time in the Word to slip. Or possibly it became routine rather than purposeful. Each one's life is a cautionary tale for leaders today.

Pastor, the most important thing in your personal life and the most essential activity in your ministry is your walk with God. Cultivate devotion to God through His Word and prayer that is meaningful and fresh, that is consistent but flexible, and that generates love for Him that protects you from temptation. Healthy pastors commune with God.

CHAPTER TWELVE

REFLECT AND DISCUSS

1. How is your communion with God? Would you describe it as routine or meaningful?

2. Have you allowed the unpredictability of a pastor's schedule to bump you out of consistent times of personal devotion? What is your plan for recovering consistency?

3. Is your communion with God growing your love for Him? In what ways? Should you adopt this purpose for your time with Him—that you will love Him more deeply and fully, resulting in persevering faithfulness and obedience?

COMPANIONSHIP IN A MINISTRY MARRIAGE

My wife Faith and I used to attend a family camp with members of our church. One of the couples' activities was a golf cart race. Each couple did a timed run through an obstacle course. The catch in this event was the husbands drove blindfolded while their wives gave them directions. What a hoot! I ran over many cones and ended up a long way from the finish line. It was a great test of how well I listened and whether I trusted my wife.

This race is pretty analogous to marriage. A couple has to learn to work together, communicating with and trusting one another to navigate through the twists and turns, avoid hazards, and make it to the finish line together. While this is true of any marriage, it's especially so of a husband and wife who are in ministry together. Ministry responsibilities and pressures strain a pastor's marriage. Subtle warning signs, if ignored, turn into marital crises.

GOD'S DESIGN

Companionship is essential to any marriage. God's original design for marriage includes this declaration: "Therefore a man shall leave his father and his mother and hold fast to his wife, and they shall become one flesh. And the man and his wife were both naked and were not ashamed" (Gen 2:24–25). "Hold fast" means to cling to, stick to, stay close. "One flesh" includes oneness on every level—circumstantial, intellectual, emotional, spiritual, and sexual.

Jesus reiterated God's design for marriage when challenged by the Pharisees about divorce: "He answered, 'Have you not read that he who created them from the beginning made them male and female, and said, "Therefore a man shall leave his father and his mother and hold fast to his wife, and the two shall become one flesh"? So they are no longer two but one flesh. What therefore God has joined together, let not man separate'" (Matt 19:4–6).

VOCATIONAL REQUIREMENT

Every husband and wife should experience companionship, but a ministry marriage has a unique need for deep and enduring oneness. In fact a strong marriage is a vocational requirement. The first qualification for pastors under the general heading "blameless" in 1 Timothy 3:2 (NKJV) is "the husband of one wife." This means he is a one-woman man, exclusively devoted to his wife. But it necessitates more than just avoiding infidelity. He fulfills God's intent for oneness with his wife.

I find this description of oneness in marriage very helpful:

> The one flesh in marriage is not just a physical phenomenon, but a uniting of the totality of two personalities. In marriage, we are one flesh spiritually by vow, economically by sharing, logistically by adjusting time and agreeing on the disbursement of all life's resources, experientially by trudging through the dark valleys and standing victoriously on the peaks of success, and sexually by the bonding of our bodies.[1]

This oneness is God's design for every marriage and requires perpetual attentiveness to cultivate, maintain, and protect it. Oneness in a ministry marriage demands at least as much if not more intentionality. A pastor

---

1. Louis H. Evans, Jr., *Hebrews: The Communicator's Commentary Series* (Word Publishing, 1985), 243.

and his wife are a package. Don't misunderstand me—she is not called to a position in the church. But the ministry is one vocation where the condition of your marriage qualifies or disqualifies you. It can make or break your ministry.

OCCUPATIONAL HAZARDS

Firefighters, law enforcement officers, construction workers—many occupations expose workers to danger. Ministry can be hazardous for your marriage. The pressures of pastoral work carry over into your home life and can strain your most important relationships.

One pastor and blogger captured the reality of this concern well:

> If a pastor feels the heaviness of pastoral ministry, so does the spouse. If a pastor is sad and burdened for a church member, the pastor's spouse sees that heartache and grieves in [her] own way. If a pastor is trashed and humiliated by disgruntled church members, the words and snide remarks not only hurt the pastor, they deeply cut the pastor's spouse. If a pastor feels overwhelmed by the burdens of their church to the point of burnout, the pastor's spouse must wrestle with what it means to have a spouse who comes home every night without the emotional energy to engage.

> Hear me if you are a young minister considering marriage—pastoral ministry is not a Norman Rockwell painting. Pastoral ministry will test the very bonds of your covenant marriage many, many times. When you as a pastor feel burdened, know that your spouse is feeling the same burden, sometimes in heavier ways. When you are emotionally exhausted at the end of the day and have nothing left to give to your spouse, know that they are often left feeling lonely. When you as a pastor "face daily the pressure of (your) concern for all the churches," know that you will often be tempted to not care for the one person for whom you should

care the most: your beautiful, strong, loving, caring, and sacrificial spouse.[2]

I've heard of some pastors' wives saying the attention and energy their husband gives to the church makes it seem like a mistress. Pastor, the threats to your marriage are real!

EXEMPLARY LIFE

The visibility of our marriages is another reason companionship is critical. A significant part of a pastor's ministry is modeling the Christian life to others. Peter instructed elders to "[Be] an example to the flock" (1 Pet 5:3). Every Christian marriage should picture Christ and His church, but people watch pastors and their marriages in a unique way.

Sadly, the fact that a pastor's marriage and family are on display can turn into unhealthy expectations on the part of church members. The pastor's wife and children can be scrutinized and criticized, causing tension in the family and a hardening of hearts toward church people. I read about a pastor and wife who were getting counseling for challenges they were going through in their marriage. The wife shared some of their struggles with the wife of one of the church elders. Consequently, the elders dismissed the pastor, telling him they didn't want a pastor who was getting marriage counseling.

Pastors and wives experience marital rough patches like everyone else. Certainly if there is a deep rift in their relationship they may need to take time to focus on themselves without the responsibilities of ministry. But it's unhealthy to be bound in fear of what people will think if they need help.

PRESSURE POINTS

The ways abound in which a pastor's marriage can experience pressure. The role of the shepherd includes 24/7 availability. A phone call or text

2. Paul Gibson, "How Ministry Will Test Your Marriage," Marriedpeople-churches.org, https://marriedpeoplechurches.org/how-ministry-will-test-your-marriage/.

can interrupt an evening out or a family vacation. Some people don't respect boundaries of privacy and time. Limited finances hinder a pastor and wife's ability to go out for a nice dinner or enjoy a romantic getaway. A pastor's wife feels alone when her husband is out all day, then again in the evening, or sitting by herself during every church gathering. This feeling can be intensified if her pastor husband has been engaging with people and their problems all day or evening and wants to relax at home without significant conversation. And the constant pull of our pride divides us from one another.

It may help you to have a conversation as husband and wife and identify threats to your companionship. Then be encouraged to know these challenges are common to pastors and wives. To paraphrase 1 Corinthians 10:13, "No test has overtaken **your marriage** that is not common **to pastors and wives**. God is faithful, and he will not let you be tempted beyond your ability, but with the test he will also provide the way of escape that you may be able to endure it."

WARNING SIGNS

How do you know if your oneness is suffering? Here are a few subtle signals that there is a problem with your companionship as husband and wife.

- Feeling distant—If your spouse makes comments like, "We aren't as close as we used to be," or, "I feel distant from you," take these seriously. Often a wife will express these concerns before a husband will. Rather than ignore or minimize them, open yourself up to hearing what she has to say and ask follow up questions. "I know I've been very focused on ministry responsibilities and problems lately. I'd like to hear what you're sensing and talk about how to cultivate more closeness with you."

- Shallow conversation—If you only talk about day-to-day life, family logistics, and ministry people and problems, and not about each other's joys, sorrows, and spiritual growth, companionship is declining.

- Underlying frustration and irritation—Not taking time to work through problems between each other and allowing them to pile up leads to a state of frustration and irritation with each other that produces a barrier to oneness and leads to resentment and bitterness.

- Frequent escapism—Spending disproportionate time on hobbies, scrolling social media, watching shows or playing video games rather than connecting with your spouse indicates an unhealthy disconnection with reality as well as your marriage.

- Outside attraction—If you're having romantic or sexual thoughts about or feeling attraction to someone other than your spouse, your "one-woman manness" is eroding. Or if you'd rather be at your office, out speaking, or anywhere other than with your spouse, whatever it is you're attracted to is your mistress.

Have you ever had your check engine light come on in your car, and you figured it wasn't anything really important and ignored it for months? You should take these symptoms much more seriously than that. Take immediate steps to eliminate the threats to oneness and put intentional effort into cultivating companionship in your marriage.

One time the oil light came on in my car, and I naively ignored it. I didn't realize that meant my engine was running without oil. A few minutes later we were on the side of the road with a blown engine. My neglect to stop the car and address the problem resulted in permanent damage and significant financial loss.

In addition to the warnings above, here are some "oil light" level symptoms that signal imminent danger in your marriage.

- Frequent, uncontrolled anger
- Abiding resentment
- Workaholic habits
- An emotional affair
- Indulgence in pornography

If any of these is present, get help now. Your marriage is headed for destruction, and your family and your ministry will pay an awful price.

COMPANIONSHIP PRINCIPLES

Many helpful marriage resources exist which pastors can not only connect their people to but also benefit from themselves. I don't need to cover the basics here. But I do want to present a few ideas that have helped my wife and me and that we've used to help others with companionship in ministry marriage.

Work at Sharing Your Life with Each Other

Faith and I enjoy watching professional tennis tournaments. One of the fun things to observe in a doubles match is how the partners work together. You'll often see them whispering to each other between points. During intense play each one seems to instinctively know where the other is on the court. I read about a tennis coach who teaches doubles partners to function as a unit by tying a rope around their waists. If the team is moving as one, the rope will remain taut but neither will be pulled off balance. Good doubles teams move forward, backward, and sideways in sync.[3]

What a great example of how couples should work together! We are naturally independent and self-centered. Sharing life means communicating about normal day-to-day life and decisions, problems, and crises in a humble, unhurtful way.

There's plenty of great material available on communication. And the next principle will address the need for making time to communicate. I want to bring up one issue here that pastors and wives have to grapple with

---

3. Ron Waite, "The Ten Commandments of Doubles," Tennisserver.com, https://www.tennisserver.com/turbo/turbo_08_06.html.

and that can become a point of tension between them—sharing church problems with your wife.

Balancing Communication Tensions

My wife and I struggled with this when I was a new lead pastor. We had to work through not only what was right and wise but also what was best for our marriage as well as my ministry and her role in it. I'm specifically thinking about counseling issues, church discipline situations, and interpersonal conflict between church members that you deal with as a pastor. Here are some of the areas pastors need to balance as we determine how much to share with our wives.

SHARE YOUR BURDENS WITH HER WITHOUT OVERBURDENING HER.

Our wives tend to be affected more in their emotions than we do, though in some marriages it's the reverse. If I share a heavy situation, she will feel the emotional weight to a greater degree than I do. Or I can compartmentalize my thoughts and feelings, and once we've talked about it, I move on, while she may dwell on it for hours and lose sleep thinking about it that night. Dwelling with my wife in an understanding way (see 1 Pet 3:7) necessitates that I don't just dump the ministry problems of that day on her upon arriving home.

Our wives probably want to share the weight with us, speak encouragement to us, and pray for us. That's a blessing we should welcome, while being careful not to overwhelm or discourage them.

COMMUNICATE OPENLY WITHOUT BETRAYING CONFIDENCES.

Some take the position, "We're one, so we tell each other everything." That's valid. When it comes to church people's problems, you both may feel it's best for her to be aware of what's going on in their lives. You may seek your wife's counsel. Let me give you some considerations which may limit how much you share with her.

One consideration is how negative personal information affects the way she views those people. She may have the capacity to know about their problems without being affected at all. But there's a possibility those very personal problems will come to the forefront of her mind the next time she has a conversation with them.

A related point to consider is that person may be embarrassed to know that your wife is aware of their struggles. We've experienced situations where the wife of a couple I was counseling said to my wife, "You know what's going on, right?" My wife was able to respond, "No, Dean doesn't tell me everything about people he meets with," and they were relieved to hear that. It's reassuring for people to know their pastor doesn't talk about the private issues they disclose in counseling.

PROTECT YOUR MARRIAGE RELATIONSHIP WHILE FUNCTIONING IN MINISTRY TOGETHER.

On the one hand, you may want to leave your problems at the office and enjoy being home, but your wife wants to hear how you spent your day and what's weighing you down. On the other hand, the two of you might tend to spend a disproportionate amount of time talking about ministry matters rather than communicating on a personal level about yourselves and your family. I don't know that there's a clear way to distinguish what's best for your marriage. But if either of you expresses concern that it's too little or too much of either personal or ministry talk, take time to work through it, each with great consideration for the other.

Face In so You Can Face Out

When you're dating, engaged, and newly married, you spend a lot of time talking face-to-face, enjoying romantic times together, and just having fun. As responsibilities grow, and if children fill your home, you begin facing these heavy demands on your energy, attention, and time side-by-side. This necessitates that you intentionally work at turning toward each other by making time to talk, to stay close, and to be intimate, so you can face daily life as one. You have to prioritize, plan, and protect time to just be together.

Here are some very practical recommendations for facing in:

- Connect for fifteen minutes every day. Spend uninter- rupted, undistracted time discussing issues of the day and whatever else is on your minds. My wife and I used to do this right after supper while our kids cleaned up the kitchen.

- Have a date night at least once every two weeks. When we were first married and didn't have much money, we sometimes went to McDonalds and ordered two apple pies for $1 and cups of water. It doesn't have to be fancy!

- Get away for a few days twice a year. This takes planning and costs money, but if you can pull it off, it's worth it. My wife often talks about how helpful it is for our mar- riage. You reconnect in ways that don't happen in the craziness of life. One retired pastor I know shares how he and his wife did this three to four times a year. They would leave town after church Sunday and come back on Tuesday. They finished well in ministry and are still going strong in their marriage![4]

- Pray together regularly. This can be at the start of the day, after a meal, when you go to bed, or any time that works for both of you. At one stage of my ministry, I often went home for lunch, and we prayed together after the meal. Now we do it after dinner or before bed. This unites you spiritually and keeps you aware of each other's hearts.

Grow Together, Not Apart

You've heard the sad refrain: "We just grew apart." It can happen to pas- tors and their wives. Let's say, if you have children, you're empty nesters at

---

4. These first three recommendations are from Paul Gibson, *How Ministry Will Test Your Marriage: Lessons from a Pastor,* https://www.startmarriageright. com/2017/09/ministry-will-test-marriage-lessons-pastor. Examples given are mine.

fifty-five years old and you both live to eighty. Just the two of you will be together without kids for twenty-five years—that's a lot of life! There isn't much new to discover about each other. Evenings are quiet. This stage of life also brings challenges such as caring for elderly parents, dealing with health problems, difficulties with adult children, and financial pressures as you near retirement age.

A phenomenon noted by secular psychologists is called gray divorce, which is the remarkable number of couples divorcing in their fifties and sixties. Psychology Today addresses reasons:

> Myriad circumstances underlie the meteoric rise in gray divorce over the past 30 years. In the late 1960s and 1970s, a focus on personal happiness and self-fulfillment became prominent. In subsequent decades in most industrialized countries, life expectancy significantly increased, attitudes about marriage as a lifelong institution shifted, divorce became more socially acceptable, and women joined the workforce and became more financially independent.
>
> Couples who married decades ago and have drifted apart or been unhappy for years become willing to face their differences about finances, interests, and emotional fulfillment and acknowledge their unsatisfying relationships. When they experience the empty nest syndrome as adult children leave home, they wonder what they now have in common. Infidelity and addictions often contribute to the decision to divorce. Spouses seek refuge from mental, emotional, and physical abuse. Betrayal from financial improprieties propels spouses to seek relief. People realize they are not living the dream they imagined when they married decades ago and are unhappy and unfulfilled. They look to the remaining decades ahead to pursue personal happiness.[5]

5. Ekua Hagan, "Why Divorce Among Older Couples Keeps Rising," Psychol-

This is a sad reality of the state of marriage in our world. While most of us consider it unthinkable to divorce in our later years of life, ministry marriages can drift toward mere coexistence and functional separation if one or both spouses are pursuing personal fulfillment rather than growing in selfless, sacrificial love and cultivating companionship.

This is a time to learn new things you can do together you both enjoy. Keep the communication going. Encourage each other to grow through trials. Work at praying together and sharing your spiritual growth with each other. Use the wisdom, character, and experience you've gained over a lifetime to influence and mentor others. Resolve that you will grow together, not apart.

ACTION STEPS

Start with a Conversation

This will take significant time. Plan an evening out or do it on a getaway.

Ask each other to rate the companionship you have in your marriage. Listen carefully and ask follow-up questions. Be open to hearing some hard things. Be ready to invest in your marriage.[6]

In their helpful resource, *The Pastor's Family*, the Crofts urge husbands to ask their wives, "'What would be the most helpful ways for me to serve you?' Then LISTEN. Also, circumstances change in ministry and marriage, so ask regularly. Also, be sensitive to times when she is especially busy or burdened. Lovingly help her through struggles with loneliness, tiredness, discouragement, anxiety, or fear."[7]

---

ogyToday.com, August 16, 2021, https://www.psychologytoday.com/us/blog/home-will-never-be-the-same-again/202108/why-divorce-among-older-couples-keeps-rising.

6. A pastor friend of mine asks his wife these questions weekly: How are we? How is the pace of life and ministry? What do you need from me? This is a great way to stay in touch with your wife and prompt conversation that protects and enhances companionship.

7. Brian and Cara Croft, *The Pastor's Family* (Zondervan, 2013), 100.

Identify and discuss what factors are negatively affecting your companionship right now. Share what each of you see as strengths and weaknesses in your companionship. What are you going to work on? What immediate steps will you take? How will you cultivate and maintain companionship through your current stage of life? How will you preserve and protect companionship during the stressful times of life and ministry together?

Determine if Recovery Is Needed

If ministry has eroded your companionship as husband and wife, don't be passive about it. It's time to invest in your most important relationship on earth.

Confess and seek forgiveness for ways you've been neglectful, self-centered, and allowed misplaced priorities to come between you. Be humble enough to admit these faults. I've found my wife is very forgiving when I am honest about my sin or stupidity.

Eliminate threats. Any outside relationship, escape, habit, or anything else that is coming between you needs to be radically amputated out of your life. Be ruthless, because these will take you down.

Enlist outside help if there is a deep rift or if there are chronic patterns you've tried unsuccessfully to overcome. Get over any reluctance to open up your lives to others. You are human just like your church members whom you would urge to get counsel when needed. It's great if you can have an older couple in your life you can be mentored by and go to for counsel. If you don't, prayerfully look for a counselor. Your marriage is worth the effort and, if necessary, expense.

Decide Together to Prioritize Your Marriage

Discuss what affects it negatively and steps to take. Be especially vigilant about your marriage during challenging times in church life or trials in your family. Enjoy the companionship God intended every married couple to have. Remember, you are **"heirs together of the grace of life!"** (1 Pet 3:7 NKJV).

CHAPTER THIRTEEN
REFLECT AND RESPOND

On your own:

1. On a scale of one to five, one being almost non-existent and five being almost perfect, how would you rate your companionship with your wife?

2. Honestly identify any warning signs that indicate your companionship with your wife is suffering. Pray for wisdom in addressing these.

3. What companionship principles stand out to you as needing attention?

4. What action steps stand out as immediate steps you should take?

With your wife:

5. Use the suggested topics under the first action step, "Start with a conversation."

TAKING A PERSONAL RETREAT

REASONS FOR A RETREAT

It is better to be proactive than reactive in dealing with busyness, stress, and exhaustion. Rather than waiting until symptoms of burnout surface in his life, a wise man in ministry will implement practices that will enable him to grow and thrive while bearing the heavy burdens of pastoral responsibility.

One of the best ways a pastor can enjoy deep and sweet fellowship with God and maintain a strong, rich preaching ministry is to take a personal retreat regularly. A time away for prayer, study, and planning can produce renewed energy, a refreshed spirit, and fruitful study that will significantly strengthen a pastor's personal life and public ministry.

Scriptural Reasons

Jesus set the example. Mark 1:35 records of Jesus Christ that, "rising very early in the morning, while it was still dark, he departed and went out to a desolate place, and there he prayed." He did this after expending physical and spiritual energy in preaching and in ministering to the needs of individual people.

Jesus regularly retreated for the express purpose of prayer (see Mark 6:46, Matt 14:23, Luke 6:12, Luke 22:39–42). He encouraged His disciples, "'Come away by yourselves to a desolate place and rest a while.' For many were coming and going, and they had no leisure even to eat" (Mark 6:31).

The apostles established priorities for preachers of all time when they said, "It is not right that we should give up preaching the word of God to serve tables. . . . But we will devote ourselves to prayer and to the ministry of the word" (Acts 6:2, 4). Both our Master and the first church leaders drew away from the busyness of ministry activity in order to devote themselves to prayer and preparation for preaching.

Practical Reasons

It is nearly impossible to give sustained attention to prayer and study in the midst of a regular schedule. Routine tasks, pressing projects, and the endless needs of people demand your time and concentration. Even when you steal away to pray, you must often get up from your knees before you are truly finished communing with your Lord. You may shut the door of your office to study, but there are a hundred distractions around you. You often close your Bible and put your notes away knowing that another hour or two of continued study might have yielded clearer understanding of the text and enabled you to capture its meaning in words potent for preaching.

When you retreat for several days, you can indulge your passion for prayer and appetite for study. Not having a tight schedule frees you to enjoy the adventure of investigating the eternal truths of God's Word. You can go much deeper and farther than you are able within the confines of your daily routine.

Other Considerations

A *good average time frame* for a personal retreat is about two to three days. Spending at least one night away allows you to settle in and get started, then sleep on what you have accomplished. You can then awake refreshed and ready to go further and dig deeper. Three days and two nights is optimal, affording you a block of time that allows for unhurried prayer, thorough study, quiet meditation, sufficient rest, and even some refreshing exercise. Frequency varies by personal preference, but consider going two to four times a year.

The *right environment* makes a personal retreat especially productive. Neither the church nor home works well for this. There are too many interruptions and distractions. If someone in your congregation offers you the use of a second house, a cabin, an apartment, or other vacant residence, consider yourself blessed! If you live near a Christian camp or retreat center, there may be a room there that you can use. There are ministries around the country that provide retreat accommodations for people in ministry, often with very economical rates, some even at no cost. Look and pray for some unique, out of the way place where you can meet with the Lord.

GOALS FOR A RETREAT

There are several different goals a pastor may have for his personal retreat. They may include long range planning for the church, personal spiritual renewal, seeking direction for a specific decision or problem, and others. As you begin your retreat, write out your specific goals. This will help you to plan your schedule.

One very profitable goal for a personal retreat is extensive studying and planning for preaching. If this is your goal, spend significant time praying for the Lord to lead you to the passages He wants you to preach from and the subjects you should emphasize in your preaching ministry. Then do background study, gain general knowledge about the book or section of Scripture you will be preaching from, and begin spadework in some of the passages. You can plan your sermon texts and topics for months in advance. Circumstances later may require you to adjust, but it is better to have to change your plan than to have no plan at all.

TYPES OF SCHEDULES

There are two different kinds of schedules that I have followed on a personal retreat. One is very structured, with blocks of time for prayer, meditation, study, and even meals, rest, and exercise. I put a copy of the schedule where I can refer to it and pace my work accordingly. That way I accomplish my goals and avoid wasting time on distractions.

The other approach one can use is to not have a schedule. Begin praying and meditating on Scripture, and let God speak. As you find yourself concentrating on certain passages, begin digging into them. As you are drawn to certain truths, pursue them. Open your heart to the personal ministry of the Holy Spirit to you. Meet with God!

MATERIALS

You will want to have all the necessary materials with you for a profitable time away. Your retreat checklist should include your Bible, key reference books you often use, commentaries on passages you may be studying, computer, pads, pens, highlighters, paper clips, sticky notes, and your personal journal. Don't forget to take some good coffee or other favorite drink that helps you think!

AN INVESTMENT

The idea of a personal retreat may seem like a luxury. Some may wonder how it is possible to fit it into their already crammed calendar. Pastors who are conscientious about their use of time and money may feel guilty. Who can justify the expense of going away in order to be alone?

The truth is, if you schedule a block of time for intense prayer, study, and planning, you are making an investment that will prove extremely productive later. You will be spiritually and mentally invigorated. There will be noticeable purpose, precision, depth, and passion in your preaching. Rather than feeling like you are behind in your study each week, you will be encouraged by knowing that you have already done significant preliminary work. You will have the confidence that comes from really praying for God's direction for your preaching ministry and responding to the Holy Spirit's leading.

Take a personal retreat. Your heart will be filled and your people will be blessed.[1]

---

1. A sabbatical is another potentially healthy practice. I have not addressed it in *The Healthy Pastor*, but I know a few men in ministry who have taken one with

CHAPTER FOURTEEN
REFLECT AND DISCUSS

1. Read the passages describing Jesus's personal retreats listed at the beginning of the chapter and his instruction to the disciples in Mark 6:31. Do you view these as examples to follow? Why or why not?

2. Think about possible goals for a personal retreat. What would you choose as your primary goal for a retreat and why?

3. What steps would you need to take to plan a retreat? Prayerfully consider taking a few of these steps.

---

benefit. Anywhere from four to eight weeks away from regular responsibilities can allow for physical rest, spiritual renewal, and if necessary, recovery from intense pressure. A sabbatical can also be a means of proactively staying spiritually, mentally, emotionally, and physically healthy to sustain a pastor through the rigors of decades of ministry work.

CONTROLLING YOUR TIME

If you don't control your time, someone else will. Managing time is a critical element of stewarding your personal resources for effective long-term ministry. Having a servant's heart doesn't mean your time belongs to everyone else. Also, as a pastor you probably don't punch a clock, so to speak, so you have a lot of unplanned hours which are easily squandered if not managed well.

To a business person, time is money. For a Christian, time is treasure, and you will either waste it or invest it wisely to please your Master. If you don't steward the resource of time, you will not have what you need to meet your responsibilities. It is up to you to determine your priorities and decide how you will utilize time to achieve your ministry objectives.

A recent study of one thousand Protestant pastors in the US showed that 51 percent of them saw time management as one of the most pressing issues they needed to address.[1] "Many pastors worry about their time management skills and how they can balance all the responsibilities they have at church and at home. In their personal lives, half of U.S. Protestant pastors say they need to focus on time management, and more than half say avoiding overcommitment is a challenge for them."[2] The pressure these

---

1. Aaron Earls, "U.S. Pastors Identify Their Greatest Needs," Research.Lifeway.com, January 11, 2022. https://research.lifeway.com/2022/01/11/u-s-pastors-identify-their-greatest-needs/.

2. Aaron Earls, "Pastors Report Struggling with Time Management, Over-Com-

pastors feel comes from "expectations from others as well as self-imposed demands."[3] One-third of the pastors surveyed said time management is the single greatest need in their personal lives.[4]

How about you? Are you in control of your time? Let's look at guiding principles and practical steps for stewardship in this critical area.[5]

HAVING RIGHT MOTIVATION

Why should you be proactive rather than allow circumstances of the day to determine how you spend your time?

First, because you are responsible to manage your resources in order to glorify God and serve others. This is, after all, why you are in ministry.

Peter made it clear that we are to use our abilities and opportunities for these purposes.

> As each has received a gift, use it to serve one another, as good stewards of God's varied grace: whoever speaks, as one who speaks oracles of God; whoever serves, as one who serves by the strength that God supplies—in order that in everything God may be glorified through Jesus Christ. To him belong glory and dominion forever and ever. Amen. (1 Pet 4:10–11)

Notice he calls us "stewards"—managers entrusted with another's resources. We have been entrusted with gifts and the opportunities to use them to fulfill divinely prescribed objectives.

Whether your gifts fall in the category of speaking (communicating God's Word) or serving (facilitating God's work), you are responsible to

---

mitment," Research.lifeway.com, April 12, 2022, https://research.lifeway.com/2022/04/12/pastors-report-struggling-with-time-management-over-commitment/.

3. Ibid.

4. Ibid.

5. An exceptional resource on personal time management and productivity from a Christian perspective is Tim Challies's *Do More Better: A Practical Guide to Productivity* (Challies, 2015).

utilize them to serve others and exalt God. Pastors often have gifts in each category. How important it is for us to follow this instruction to steward our resources. Our motivation is not merely to be productive, or efficient, or present a persona of being organized. Stewardship of time enables us to fulfill the highest goal of glorifying God and the secondary goal of truly ministering to others.

Another motivation is good time management enables us to seize opportunities to do God's will. Paul highlighted this in Ephesians 5:15–17: "Look carefully then how you walk, not as unwise but as wise, making the best use of the time, because the days are evil. Therefore do not be foolish, but understand what the will of the Lord is."

Managing time well also pleases our Master. To each servant who invested his talents wisely in Jesus's parable recorded in Matthew 25, the master spoke these glowing words: "Well done, good and faithful servant. You have been faithful over a little; I will set you over much. Enter into the joy of your master" (Matt 25:21).

One more helpful motivation is to accomplish things that matter. Organization requires self-discipline. Like with physical exercise, music practice, or learning a language, if you're motivated, you'll be disciplined. Our highest motivation for self-discipline is eternal. Paul argued this in 1 Corinthians 9:24–27:

> Do you not know that in a race all the runners run, but only one receives the prize? So run that you may obtain it. Every athlete exercises self-control in all things. They do it to receive a perishable wreath, but we an imperishable. So I do not run aimlessly; I do not box as one beating the air. But I discipline my body and keep it under control, lest after preaching to others I myself should be disqualified.

The discipline of controlling your time is worth it because it provides opportunities for us to accomplish eternal work.

KEEPING PERSPECTIVE

A few important concepts to keep in mind when working at time management are, first, stay submitted to God's will and flexible with plans. I often plan how I'm going to spend a day in ministry or at home. Sometimes the plan actually happens! There's a right balance between controlling how we spend our time and adjusting to circumstances beyond our control. James's reality check is helpful: "Come now, you who say, 'Today or tomorrow we will go into such and such a town and spend a year there and trade and make a profit'—yet you do not know what tomorrow will bring. What is your life? For you are a mist that appears for a little time and then vanishes. Instead you ought to say, 'If the Lord wills, we will live and do this or that'" (Jas 4:13–15).

Second, we need to recognize others may view time and tasks differently. Some people groups and local cultures are less time and task oriented and more people and relationship oriented. We should all learn the culture where God has placed us and be considerate of those we minister to rather than forcing our practices on them. We can still work at using our time wisely while not being overbearing in our demeanor toward others.

Third, people are more important than projects. Some of us are more task oriented than people focused. We can set our agenda for the week with the goal of accomplishing the to-dos of ministry and neglect the very essence of ministry, which is to influence other people toward knowing God and serving Christ. The shepherd might forget about the sheep.

A good practice for the pastor who tends to be task and project focused is to look over the upcoming week and intentionally include planned times to be with people, including pastoral visits as well as evangelistic and discipleship appointments. I heard a seasoned pastor say that ministry is not about getting projects done, but about getting people done. That helpful maxim fits with Paul's motivation for laboring hard in ministry—"that we may present everyone mature in Christ" (Col 1:28).

Now the converse may be true as well—a pastor may be so attentive to people that he neglects important tasks. He may need to proactively include time slots for accomplishing the to-dos of ministry.

KNOWING YOUR MISSION

A major step in wisely using time is determining your mission in life and ministry. What does God want you to do with your life? Can you state it in a sentence? Pray about it, search the Scriptures, and brainstorm.

Consider your gifts, desires, opportunities, and compelling burdens. Who has God made you to be? How has He gifted you? What are your strengths? What do you want to do?

Think about where God has placed you now and what you are supposed to be doing there. He providentially places you in your community, your church, your family. What is your role in those places?

I have found that stating my personal mission has helped me establish corresponding priorities and practices, especially in how I use my time. For example, my simple mission statement when I pastored was "Shepherd the flock God has entrusted to my care." Now it is "Equip a new generation of pastors, be a friend to men in ministry, and encourage biblical church growth." Of course you can include wording pertinent to your role as husband and father as well, such as "Love my wife, nurture my children, and . . ." Having a clear sense of mission not only helps me plan my time but also provides a guide for saying yes or no to requests by others for commitments of my time.

IDENTIFYING YOUR ROLES AND RESPONSIBILITIES

Since I am primarily addressing pastors, this should be fairly easy. But you may have a specific role within a pastoral team or church context, such as lead pastor, pastor of discipleship, or youth and family pastor. What set of responsibilities comes with your role? Try to state them in three to five bullet points that can guide your decisions about use of time.

UNDERSTANDING KEY COMPONENTS

Now we come to the practical aspects of being organized with your time. Three main components are involved.

Your Schedule

Your schedule is your commitment of time. Think of your time like your checking account. You receive your salary in the form of a set amount of money directly deposited into your account every month. You budget how you're going to spend it.

It's the same with time. We all receive a set amount, and our schedule reflects how we plan to spend it. If you don't have a budget for your finances, you'll likely spend it impulsively, a lot of other people will end up with your money, and you won't have what you need to pay your bills. If you don't plan how to spend your time, the same will happen—it will get eaten up by social media, people who want to shoot the breeze, and a thousand other things. Either you control your time or someone else will, and your schedule reflects your priorities and commitments.

Tasks

Tasks are your commitment of energy as well as time. Some tasks are determined for you. But you can determine tasks you will perform every day based on your mission, priorities, and responsibilities.

Information

Information provides resources for fulfilling your mission. Information comes to you in the form of emails, texts, documents, videos, old-fashioned snail mail, and more. These require you to make a decision, formulate a response, or store them for ready access when needed.

Sometimes our roles expand, and we take on additional responsibilities, or we are moved to another level of leadership and have more people in our scope of ministry. When this happens, the schedule, tasks, and information we have to manage grow exponentially. You have to manage these, or your life will be chaotic and stress-filled, leading to burnout. In order to manage these key components, you need a systematic approach.

SELECTING THE TOOLS

I was in college when I started intentionally managing my time. Each day I wrote my class schedule and other appointments on a 3 x 5 card, along with a list of to-dos for the day. On the other side of the card I wrote a Bible verse I wanted to meditate on that day. Later I graduated to a professionally produced planner system. I currently use a digital calendar in combination with a paper journal for my task list and meeting notes.[6]

There is a myriad of options, including both digital and hard copy versions of time, task, and information management resources. The key is finding out what works for you and which may change with your role, responsibilities, setting, and preference for paper or technology.

DEVELOPING DISCIPLINED PRACTICES

You can have the latest app, the classiest leather planner, and the best intentions, but discipline is the key to any time management system. You have to work at it. One way I challenge my pastoral students to think about the necessity for discipline with time management is this: If you don't manage your time well, you will put that burden on someone else. Being irresponsible makes someone else responsible. Becoming an adult is taking responsibility for yourself so others don't have to.

Pastor, you don't want others in your ministry, whether leaders or church members, to have to take up your slack. Here are some disciplined practices that have helped me. Consider these and develop your own that fit your role, personality, and place of ministry.

---

6. *Unique: The Ultimate Planner for Creative Professionals* is designed by Phil Cooke and includes space for a daily prioritized task list, important calendar items, and a full dot grid page for meeting notes and creative thinking. One very helpful feature is the blank date line so you can use it only on the days you need it and not waste pages. See philcooke.com/unique-creative-planner/.

Disciplines for Managing Your Time with a Calendar

- Write it down. The pastor who mentored me in ministry repeated a quote: "The faintest ink is more powerful than the strongest memory." Immediately enter appointments in your calendar. Don't rely on your memory. I've heard pastors bemoan the criticism they received when they missed appointments with church members because they didn't put it on their calendar. Set reminders if you aren't naturally time conscious. Be punctual. Respect other people's time.

- Make appointments with yourself. Schedule projects or tasks that are high priority or that you know will take significant time. I would definitely include sermon preparation in this. If someone asks you to do something else, you can honestly say, "I have a commitment at that time." Of course if it's urgent, you can adjust, but usually you can find another time to meet their need.

- Check your calendar before scheduling anything new rather than trusting your memory to avoid overbooking or double-booking. Learn to say no or "I'm not able to do that this week but how about next week?"

- A helpful practice is to go over your calendar at the beginning of each week so you know what's coming up, and coordinate with your spouse as needed. Also check your calendar at the end of each day to be aware of what's happening the next day.

- Confirm appointments by text or email, especially if they're made weeks in advance. This ensures you and the other party are both planning on it, and the time and place are set.

- Use minutes, not just hours. Learn to work on a task, make a call, send a text or email in a brief slice of time you have between other commitments.

- If you're task oriented, intentionally plan time with people.

Disciplines for Managing Your Responsibilities with a Task List

- Again, write it down. Enter every task on a master list. This can be done monthly or weekly. Using a master list declutters your mind and ensures you don't forget something important.

- Make a daily task list at the beginning of each day or the end of the previous day. Enter items from your master list as well as other tasks that come up.

- Prioritize your daily tasks. I can't say enough about how energizing this practice is. Number each task in the order you plan to do it, usually based on what you must accomplish that day. This ensures you give attention to the tasks in order of importance. You can also number them in an order that fits the time slots you have that day.

- Schedule times during the day when you will work on these tasks—either blocks of time or specific time slots for specific tasks.

- When you have a few minutes of down time, check the task list and see if you can complete any of them.

- Track the progress of tasks by how you mark them. I learned this system from Franklin Planner—a checkmark for completion, a dot if it's in progress, (e.g., sent an email and waiting for response), a circle with an initial if it's been delegated, and an arrow if you move it forward to another day.[7]

- Treat email as either a task or a calendar commitment.

- Update your list daily. Move uncompleted tasks from the previous day to another day.

Disciplines for Managing Information with Files

- Have a place for all kinds of information you receive. Set up physical and digital files for documents related to your roles and responsibilities.

- Practice TRAF when dealing with written material. Every time you handle a piece of information, decide if you will Toss, Refer (send or delegate it to someone else), Act on it, or File it.

- Clean your files out yearly and keep only what is necessary.

COMMUNICATING WITH YOUR PEOPLE

Sometimes church leaders and members need help understanding why time management is important for a pastor. Of course you don't want to send a wrong message of isolation or inaccessibility. Assure them of your care for them as well as your desire to serve the Lord faithfully.

I suggest saying something like this: "I strive to be a good steward of my time. My responsibilities include the ministry of the Word, caring spiritually for our people, and overseeing the church spiritually and organizationally. I endeavor to fulfill these best I am able. My mornings are set aside for studying the Word and preparing to preach. If you call or text me, I may not be able to respond immediately. I care about you and will as soon as I'm able."

---

7. "Task Symbols," Franklinplanner.com, September 15, 2016, https://blog.franklinplanner.com/task-symbols/.

Ideally you can set up a number of people who can process emergency calls, such as an administrative assistant, pastoral team member or elder, or a deacon. Let your people know one of these can reach you if there's a true emergency.

PLANNING TIME AWAY

Controlling your time includes prioritizing, scheduling, and protecting periods when you are out from under the responsibilities of ministry.

Start with a weekly day off. Plan it, schedule it, take it, and stick with it.

Take an annual extended vacation. Two weeks is optimal. Don't wait until your wife threatens to take a beach trip by herself. Don't believe the lie that you should be able to keep going without a break. Don't let fear of the church falling apart without you keep you from getting away for a couple of weeks. They'll miss you, but that's not a bad thing. They'll survive, and both you and the church will be better for it.

Get away overnight once or twice a year with just your wife. Your marriage needs it. When my wife and I do this, we're amazed at how we reconnect with each other in just a day or two away. This was especially true when our kids were at home but is still surprisingly true as empty nesters.

Attend an annual conference. You need to listen and to be fed.

Scripture reminds us our lives flow by at a rapid pace. In contrast to our God who exists "from everlasting to everlasting" (Ps 90:2), our lives are like grass—"in the morning it flourishes" but "in the evening it fades and withers" (vv. 5–6). Seventy years is considered a full life (v. 10), and we should calculate, not just the number of years, but how many days we have left (v. 12). Try it! Subtract your current age from 70, then multiply by 365. You can add in a day for each leap year if you want to be precise. I did this recently and was surprised by how low that number seemed. It's sobering!

Controlling your time doesn't eliminate enjoyment of life! But it is an important part of stewarding your personal life so you can serve our God all your days.

REFLECT AND DISCUSS

1. How does the concept of stewardship help you think about your use of time?

2. What is your personal mission in life and ministry? In what ways should you adjust your use of time in order to fulfill your mission more effectively?

3. Are there tools or disciplines you should implement to be a better steward of your time? Which ones, and how do you plan to put them into practice?

CHAPTER SIXTEEN

HOLY DISTRACTIONS

My wife says I'm a hobby person. I suppose that's true. When I was a little boy, my brother-in-law, who collected all kinds of things, started me on collecting postmarks. That was when local post offices hand stamped mail with their unique postmark including the town and date. The first hobby I remember taking up on my own was fishing. I suppose that's just a normal boyhood activity for many, but it turned into more of a pursuit later in life when I discovered the sweet joy of trout fishing in the freestone rivers and mountain streams flowing down from the Blue Ridge escarpment bordering North and South Carolina.

My most recent hobby is beekeeping. It was beekeeping that got me thinking about hobbies in the life of a pastor. One day I stumbled across a journal article titled, "Bee-Keeping as Holy Distraction in the Life of the Revd Charles Butler, 1571–1647." The author observed that, remarkably, the men known as "the father of English beekeeping" (Charles Butler), "the father of Irish beekeeping" (Joseph Diggs), and "the father of American beekeeping" (Lorenzo Langstroth) were all clergymen.

Butler published one of the first beekeeping manuals in English, *The Feminine Monarchie* (1623). Diggs published *The Practical Bee Guide* in 1910. Langstroth wrote *The Hive and the Honey Bee* (1853), and his name is attached to the modern hive design that is used by most beekeepers today, including large-scale commercial honey producers with thousands of hives. All of these were pastors!

The journal article observes, "Learning and longevity attended [Butler], to which qualities bee-keeping may well have had a contributory factor" and that "Langstroth and Digges also made bee-keeping a significant interest in their working lives, which contributed to their well-being. For Langstroth, it provided a sense of healing after ill health and stress; for Digges, there was an unalloyed sense of happiness in relating to bees; for Butler, the appreciation of bees contributed to his appreciation of the wonder of Creation."[1]

The positive effects on these men bear repeating: learning, longevity, well-being, healing after sickness and stress, happiness, and appreciation of the wonders of creation. I can echo all of those testimonies. A good friend knew I was trying to get into beekeeping at the same time I was going through a season of intense personal pain. He showed up at my house one day with a package of bees.[2] He said he hoped beekeeping would be therapeutic for me, and he wanted to help me get started. His desire has proven true.

How does the topic of hobbies fit with pastoral health? Here's a down-to-earth illustration. A friend told me a story about a pastor who liked to work in his garden early in the morning.

> One day a parishioner happened to walk out of the nearby woods where he had been bowhunting for deer. With a disapproving look, he asked the pastor why he was wasting time in his garden when he could be in his study preparing Sunday's sermon. The pastor responded with a question, "When you put your bow away, do you keep it strung?"
>
> "No, it would ruin the bow," the hunter replied.

---

1. John Owen, "Bee-keeping as Holy Distraction in the Life of the Revd Charles Butler, 1571–1647," *Rural Theology*, 16(2): 132–135, October 3, 2018, https://www.tandfonline.com/doi/full/10.1080/14704994.2018.1519908.

2. A package of bees is a screened box containing two to three pounds of worker bees and a queen for starting a new hive.

"Same with me," said the pastor. "If the tension is always on, I'll wear out and not be able to last in ministry."

As we've established in earlier chapters, ministry is a high stress occupation. If the tension of ministry is always on your mind, body, and soul, you will wear down and lose your effectiveness. Hobbies and outside pursuits are ways to release the tension that comes with the rigors of ministry so you can be renewed and ready to serve again.

Hobbies also cultivate your mind, strengthen your body, and elevate your soul in ways that make you a healthier person. Sure, having a hobby is not a primary essential to pastoral longevity like guarding your integrity or companionship in your marriage. But it is an element of human experience that can enhance your well-being and extend your effectiveness in ministry.

Christian author and blogger Tim Challies was asked in an interview, "How should pastors think about passions or hobbies outside of ministry?" I think his response provides a good perspective:

> One of the temptations for a pastor is to make an idol out of his ministry, to give all his time to that ministry, even at the expense of his own soul or his own health or his own family. So, I'd want to be careful as a pastor that I wasn't so committed to that, that I was going to wreck my own life for the ministry. And many, many pastors would attest that they've done that. So, don't make an idol out of the ministry. And, one of the ways you can do that is by having time for other passions, other pursuits. So, if reading is a passion, if writing is a passion, then taking time, deliberately carving out time to give to that will actually make you a better pastor because it will be relaxing, it will be fostering a different, something else, a different interest in your life.[3]

---

3. Tim Challies, "How Can You Balance Life and Ministry and Your Passions and Hobbies?" Challies.com, vlog transcript, October 4, 2018, https://www.challies.com/vlog/how-can-you-balance-life-and-ministry-and-your-passions-

To be sure we're thinking together, a hobby is defined as "an activity you do for pleasure when you are not working."[4] I would add the idea of something you do regularly, not just once or a couple of times.

Our definition of pastoral health is "stewardship of your physical life and cultivation of your inner man in order to most effectively fulfill your calling to shepherd the flock of God." A healthy pastor is physically well and has a thriving soul. Let's explore the idea of hobbies and how they can contribute to long-term ministry for the glory of God.

A BIBLICAL BASIS FOR HOBBIES IN THE LIFE OF A PASTOR

I'm not aware of biblical instruction that directs us to have hobbies. But there are a few texts that support the idea that all of life isn't work, and we are justified in having pleasurable pursuits outside of our primary calling and daily work.

First Corinthians 10:31 says, "Whether you eat or drink or whatever you do, do all to the glory of God." We can engage in mundane activities, including hobbies, that have the potential for glorifying God.

We are told in 1 Corinthians 6:19–20 that "your body is the temple of the Holy Spirit" and to "glorify God in your body." The context addresses the sin of sexual immorality. We show our high view of God by abstaining from sinning with the bodies He gave us and that He Himself indwells. By implication, the positive side is we can show our high view of God by doing things in our physical bodies that He commands. I would add that we can glorify Him by experiencing legitimate pleasures He created our bodies with the capacity to enjoy. Hobbies can be in this category.

In 1 Timothy 6:17, Paul instructed Timothy to challenge materially prosperous Christians not to place confidence in their possessions but

---

and-hobbies.

4. *Cambridge Dictionary Online*, s.v. "hobby," https://dictionary.cambridge.org/us/dictionary/english/hobby.

rather in God. In this context He described God as the one who "richly provides us with all things to enjoy." The implication is God has filled the world with legitimate, pleasurable experiences, and enjoying them is a way to glorify Him as our good and gracious heavenly Father. Hobbies are often ways to enjoy the riches of God's world.

Charles Butler quoted Psalm 111:2 at the end of his book on beekeeping: "Great are the works of the Lord, studied by all who delight in them." I can personally attest to the opportunity beekeeping gives me to witness divine design. My observation and study of those little creatures often brings me to worship. A hobby can lead us to delight in the works of our Lord and elevate our hearts to praise Him.

BENEFITS OF HOBBIES IN THE LIFE OF A PASTOR

Where do I start? The benefits are numerous. Or at least I think so, since I'm a hobby person. But my position is backed by research: "Numerous studies demonstrate the mental and physical health benefits of having a hobby or interest outside of work, even if your work is ministry."[5] What are some of these benefits? I've compiled a few.

- Hobbies provide temporary relief from weighty issues enabling you to re-engage later with greater concentration and clarity. When your mind is engaged, often your body is not. You're sitting at a desk with little or no physical exertion taking place. But when your body is at work, your mind is at rest, or at least not focused intently on study, planning, counseling, or some other mental endeavor. Physical activity shifts your energy so your thoughts can flow freely. This actually may bene-

---

5. Aaron Earls, "Why Pastors Need Hobbies," Research.lifeway.com, June 22, 2022, https://research.lifeway.com/2022/06/22/why-pastors-need-hobbies/. The article does not substantiate this claim, but another article that cites such "numerous studies" is by Emma Parkhurst, "How Hobbies Improve Mental Health," Utah State University, October 25, 2021, https://extension.usu.edu/mentalhealth/articles/how-hobbies-improve-mental-health.

fit the work side of your life, because when your mind is free, you tend to think creatively and sometimes develop a plan, gain an insight, or solve a problem when you aren't even trying.

• Hobbies and outside pursuits often involve physical activity that combats stress and brings greater health. Whether you're working out or just moving around while you engage in your hobby, it's better for you than sitting. If you count steps, you'll likely get more than when you're at your desk. Just getting outdoors and going for a walk can reenergize you and clear your mind. I love Charles Spurgeon's words on this. His *Lectures To My Students* includes a chapter on "The Minister's Fainting Fits," in which he wrote:

> Sedentary habits have a tendency to create despondency in some constitutions. . . . To sit long in one posture, poring over a book, or driving a quill, is in itself a taxing of nature; but add to this a badly ventilated chamber, a body which has long been without muscular exercise, and a heart burdened with many cares, and we have all the elements for preparing a seething cauldron of despair, especially in the dim months of fog.[6]

> He encourages walks in nature, which I love and always find refreshing. He says, "The ferns and the rabbits, the streams and the trouts, the fir trees and the squirrels, the primroses and the violets, the farm-yard, the new-mown hay, and the fragrant hops—these are the best medicine for hypochondriacs, the surest tonics for the declining, the best refreshments for the weary."[7]

6. C. H. Spurgeon, *Lectures to My Students* (Marshall, Morgan and Scott, Ltd., reprinted 1982), 157–158.

7. Ibid., 158.

Whether a hobby or just something you do on a break, do yourself a favor and go for a walk!

- As one writer says, "Hobbies can give us a tangible activity to start and finish in a pastoral world of unending to-dos and of long term investment in people's lives."[8] Ministry requires intense mental and spiritual labor. The work of making disciples is endless. When Sunday's over, or at the end of any day, there is still more people work to be done. I think this is why some pastors enjoy mowing their lawn on Mondays. It's attainable, measurable, and visible. You can stand on your front porch or back deck and view the completed job with immediate satisfaction. The same is true with building a piece of furniture out of wood or catching a nice fish. There it is in your hands. Job done.

- Hobbies help you connect with people as friends. In ministry, you're always on. You can't to go church, or maybe even out to eat, without being in pastor mode. A hobby can place you in a casual setting where pastoring isn't your primary function. The people you're with are focused on the activity more than on each other's work. If your role as a pastor comes up, sure, it may provide an opportunity to speak of Christ. The same would be true of any Christian. But you can make personal connections and develop friendships as a man, which is healthy.[9]

- Some hobbies give you time to pray and worship in the beauty and majesty of creation. Hunting at sunrise, kayaking across a glassy lake or down powerful rapids, feeling the sun on your neck or the rain against your skin,

8. Rusty McKie, "Pastors and the Hobby-less Life," Amicalled.com, July 6, 2017. https://amicalled.com/pastors-and-the-hobby-less-life/.

9. Some of these ideas are from McKie, "Pastors and the Hobby-less Life."

witnessing the flashing leap of a rainbow trout on your line, walking to your ball on a tree-lined fairway, pulling that bird in close with your binoculars—so many ways to experience and enjoy the handiwork of our great God. I have my best prayer times on a walk or bike ride or while standing in a river with fishing rod in hand.

- Some sources I've read bring out the gospel influence you can have on unbelievers through hobbies. I don't think everything we do has to turn into evangelism. But connecting with people who are without Christ can certainly happen through hobbies, and we should always be ready to take those opportunities.

- Another possible benefit is the opportunity to help and serve others. You can share your products, your knowledge, or your skills in ways that are a blessing to others. While I sell some of my honey to support my beekeeping habit, I also give some away as I have opportunity and feel led.

- Hobbies provide sermon illustrations. We can draw many examples and analogies from our areas of interest. However, we should use a variety of sources so our people don't roll their eyes when we tell another golf, fishing, or fill-in-your-hobby story.

- Hobbies make you a relatable person. Pastors are often viewed as living on a different plane from normal people, especially by those who don't go to church. When someone finds out you have interests that go with being human, they perceive you as more on their level. Hobbies make great conversation topics. Once people find out you do something especially interesting, they ask you questions about it. Just don't bore them to death! Turn the conversation around and find out what they do for fun too.

Nearly half of pastors have a hard time taking time for hobbies or other interests outside of their ministry work.[10] I was talking with some pastors at a conference about deer hunting. One pastor's comment revealed how many of us think: "Why do we feel guilty about taking time to go hunting?" I responded with one thought: "The ministry is endless. There's always more work to do."

I think another reason we feel guilty about hobbies is we don't want to be thought of as lazy, especially since we don't clock in and out of our job. It might feel like a waste of time, or we're concerned others will view it that way. Hopefully, seeing these benefits will help you consider developing outside pursuits without feeling like you're doing something wrong. They are not inherently a waste of time and can help you personally as well as enhance your relationships with others.

CAUTIONS ABOUT HOBBIES IN THE LIFE OF A PASTOR

I can think of a few ways that pastors should be cautious about hobbies. Probably the most obvious is outside pursuits can become more of a time commitment than they should. Balancing our priorities is an essential practice. Communion with God, companionship with your wife, involvement with your children, and pastoral work fill up most of your schedule. You fit hobbies in where you can.

Another area of caution is using hobbies as a way to escape the responsibilities of life and ministry. We can't let them become a habitual escape from daily work or family life. If you do hobby-related internet searches during hours dedicated to sermon preparation, or head out to your woodworking shop when you need to have a difficult conversation with your wife or one of your children, that may be a sign you are using it as an escape.

---

10. Earls, "Why Pastors Need Hobbies."

Another caution relates to how your leisure activity affects your relationship with your wife. If any outside pursuit creates conflict between you, it's time for a heart-to-heart talk about why. She may feel you are spending an inordinate amount of time, money, physical or emotional energy, or mental bandwidth on your hobby. Listen carefully to her concerns and move toward unity and agreement about your stewardship of these resources.

One more caution is that it might be possible to focus your heart's passion on an activity, possession, or experience in a way that should be reserved for God. Some experiences appeal strongly to the pleasure centers of our brains. Endorphin release is a real thing and can result in enjoyable activities having an addictive power in our lives. Or we may just derive mental satisfaction in what we participate in or produce.

We find ourselves devoting time, energy, and attention to the objects or experiences associated with our hobby to the neglect or exclusion of spiritual pursuits—our communion with God and service to Him. At some point the object of our interest becomes an idol.

A word from a prominent pastor in our day can help us evaluate the place of hobbies in our lives. John Piper is famous for his exhortation to believers contained in the title of his book *Don't Waste Your Life*. Piper responded to an interview question about whether it is legitimate for a Christian to spend time and money on hobbies. His answer recognizes the legitimate place of hobbies in our lives but recommends we ask ourselves whether the activity feeds our souls with God-exalting experiences or leads us to love Him less and love the world more. He also suggests asking whether it refreshes us spiritually, emotionally, and physically for the areas of our lives where we need energy to glorify Him, or whether it depletes and weakens us. And a final question is if the hobby draws others into our lives so we can point them to Christ.[11]

---

11. John Piper, "How Hobbies Glorify God," Desiringgod.org, interview, February 4, 2014, www.desiringgod.org/interviews/how-hobbies-glorify-god.

Hobbies have their place but should be kept in order under our highest priorities and never take the place, or even distract us from, our passionate pursuit of loving God and serving Him with our lives.

IDEAS FOR HOBBIES IN THE LIFE OF A PASTOR

There are so many possibilities! I surveyed a group of pastors to find out what they do. Here's a partial list. The first few lines include more common hobbies, followed by less common and unusual ones.

Golf, fishing, hunting, reading, cycling, tennis, bowling, archery, camping, hiking, backpacking, musical instruments, video games, motorcycle riding, guns and shooting, skiing, kayaking, tinkering, woodworking, travel, reading in various genres, yard work, photography, cooking, gardening, table tennis, pickleball, sailing, white water rafting, car restoration, beekeeping, sports cards, wargaming, board games, nerdy board games, card games, watching sports, coffee roasting, water gardening, small scale entrepreneurship, computer programming, graphic design, home repair and improvement, carpentry, construction and restoration projects, learning a new language, snorkeling/scuba diving, old western movies, ATVing, reading/watching fantasy and science fiction, firewood, ham radio, watercolor painting, genealogical research, Civil War history, balloon twisting, magic tricks, pizza oven, grilling, smoking meat, coaching sports, fantasy football, skateboarding, writing music, martial arts, premium Bibles, technology, writing, disc golf, Legos, metal detecting, auto repairs, auto detailing, used book hunting, competitive cornhole, parkour, cross-stitching, videography, comic books, birding, farming, stamp collecting, model trains, snowmobiling, making bread, retro video game collecting, blacksmithing, furniture repurposing, fountain pens, word and number puzzles

Exercise might be considered a hobby if you enjoy it. One pastor said he tried a new hobby every year to see how he liked it, then decided whether to stick with it or not.

The bottom line on hobbies is that they give you an opportunity to de-stress and be refreshed in mind, body, and soul. They can make a contribution to a pastor's personal health when kept in the right balance with the priorities and responsibilities of life and ministry.

CHAPTER SIXTEEN

REFLECT AND DISCUSS

1. What are your hobbies? Which one do you enjoy the most? Why?

2. Which of the benefits of hobbies in this chapter stood out to you? Why? Which of the cautions stood out to you, and why?

3. Are there any changes you would like to make regarding hobbies? What are they?

DISCIPLINED PHYSICAL HABITS

A NEEDED PERSPECTIVE

Pastoral life, unlike actual shepherding work, is sedentary. We work long at our desks, drive to visits, and sit through so many meetings. Additionally, the stress-filled work of pastors tends to negatively affect our physical health.[1] When we're not at our best physically, our work suffers, which becomes a destructive cycle. As one pastor observed, "Poor physical health translates into less effective ministry."[2]

Some have declared an "obesity epidemic" among pastors. I want to be sensitive here, recognizing there are chronic health conditions that cause weight gain. But many of us can and should honestly face the problem. The obesity rate of pastors in America exceeds the national average of the general population—40 percent compared to 29 percent![3]

One study reports a decline in the physical health of pastors from 2015–2022, with the percentage of those who ranked their physical health as average or poor more than tripling over that time period.[4] Sixty-seven percent of pastors say their physical well-being is excellent or good, compared

---

1. The negative effect of ministry on physical health was addressed in chapter 1.

2. Burns et al., 98.

3. Proeschold-Bell and Byassee, 85–86.

4. "How Rest & Sabbath Can Strengthen Pastoral Well-Being," Barna.com, June 15, 2023, https://www.barna.com/research/rest-sabbath/.

to 88 percent regarding spiritual well-being and 85 percent emotional well-being.[5]

We've defined pastoral health as stewardship of your body and cultivation of your inner man in order to most effectively fulfill your calling to shepherd the flock of God. A healthy pastor is physically well and has a thriving soul. We addressed some aspects of physical health earlier, but it warrants more specific treatment.

Disciplined physical habits will help you be a healthy pastor. Scripture supports this. We looked earlier at John's wish for his ministry friend, Gaius, that he would "be in good health" (3 John 2). Paul describes how he is "temperate in all things" to obtain "an imperishable crown." "I discipline my body and bring it into subjection" is his testimony of maintaining physical self-discipline (1 Cor 9:25–27).

We do need to maintain the right perspective, acknowledging that "our outward man is perishing" and "the inward man is being renewed day by day" and that we should "not look at the things which are seen, but at the things which are not seen. For the things which are seen are temporary, but the things which are not see are eternal" (2 Cor 4:16–18). Our bodies are vessels we use to glorify God, not an end in themselves. We should avoid the ditch of neglecting our bodies while staying out of the other ditch of being obsessed with our physical condition.

We can all feel guilty about our lack of discipline. My purpose is to encourage you to pay attention to your physical health for the purpose of ministering effectively with longevity.

KEY COMPONENTS[6]

A Healthy Diet

The average adult needs 1800–2000 calories a day, including a balance of carbohydrates (20–30 percent), protein (40–50 percent), and good fats

---

5. Barna Group, *The State of Pastors*, 16–17.

6. Some of the following material is drawn from an interview with my friend Narasimha Palagummi, MD, who specializes in Internal Medicine and Executive Health.

(30 percent). Lean white meats are best with limited red meat included, along with sources of fiber, such as vegetables and in-season fruits. We need 60–75 ounces of water a day.

Some caffeine is healthy (up to four cups a day depending on individual metabolism), but fancy coffee shop creations with lots of sugar aren't, and it's best not to drink caffeine after 2:00 p.m.

Three meals a day is optimal with snacks mid-morning and afternoon. Breakfast is the most important meal, and dinner should be lighter since we are usually not active in the evening.

Now we know it takes discipline for anyone to maintain this kind of diet. Add the fact that pastors do not function in a healthy environment when it comes to food. One pastor accurately observed, "Church life doesn't work without food. Lots of food. Not healthy food."[7] This is compounded by the tendency to eat when stressed. No wonder only 25 percent of pastors have a normal weight.[8]

Recovery is possible, but it requires discipline. Fad diets and avoiding major food groups (such as carbohydrates) rarely work and can have negative health effects. Limiting calories, maintaining a regular meal schedule without unhealthy snacking, and exercise is the way to go.[9]

Sufficient Rest

Seven hours of sleep per night is optimal for most adults. What might disrupt this pattern for a pastor? Church issues, people's problems, and conflicts may surface in your mind as your head hits the pillow. Watching shows at night or scrolling social media in bed stimulates your mind and nervous system rather than calming you down.

You are more likely to fall asleep and enjoy a good night of rest if you have a consistent time when you go to bed and get up, at least within a one-hour range. Other relaxation inducements include exercising in the late

---

7. Proeschold-Bell and Byassee, 81.

8. Ibid., 84.

9. Ibid., 97. The authors list helpful proactive steps for a pastor's dietary health.

afternoon or evening, taking a shower before you go to bed, and avoiding technology close to bedtime. If you tend to wake up hungry, eat a small snack before bed, but avoid too much liquid. If necessary, try a low dose of melatonin. Trust the Lord with the problems that weigh on your mind. You need rest, but He "will neither slumber nor sleep" (Ps 121:4).

Regular Exercise

The recommendation for exercise is three to four periods of thirty to forty-five minutes a week including aerobic activity, such as brisk walking, jogging, cycling, or a sport to get your heart rate up. Using weights, a kettlebell, or doing pushups and pullups will help maintain strength and muscle tone.

For additional activity, set a timer when you're working at your desk and take breaks to go for a walk. Consider investing in an adjustable desk so you can stand. Take the stairs when visiting the hospital.

Medical Support

The stereotypical man won't see a doctor until EMTs wheel him into the emergency room. It's better to be proactive. A yearly screening is best practice. Your doc, your wife, and common sense will guide you in getting further help as needed.

Health and Holiness

We are stewards of the whole man. God's sanctifying work extends to all aspects of our lives. Paul prayed, "Now may the God of peace himself sanctify you completely, and may your whole spirit and soul and body be kept blameless at the coming of our Lord Jesus Christ" (1 Thess 5:23). Appropriate attention to our bodies is part of our new life in Christ. "The old life may have included slothful or obsessive activities such as inconsistent sleep habits, crazy work hours, poor or neurotic exercise, and an unhealthy diet. Self-denying self-care, on the other hand, may include getting to bed on time, saying no to work by setting aside periods for sabbath and sabbatical, getting responsible exercise, and eating a balanced diet."[10]

---

10. Burns et al., 21.

MINISTRY LONGEVITY

How many automobiles have you owned in your lifetime? I think I've had ten or more. When the mileage reaches a certain point, or when it's damaged beyond repair, we junk it or trade it for another one. Think of your physical body as the vehicle you've been given for carrying out the work to which God has called you. Unlike your cars, you only get one to last you a lifetime. Some people take such good care of their cars that they can drive them for decades. It makes sense to take care of our bodies so we can enjoy a long life of ministry.

REFLECT AND DISCUSS

1. Do you normally observe a healthy diet? Does anything need to change?

2. Are you getting enough sleep? If not, what can you do to get better rest?

3. What are your exercise habits? If inadequate, how can you improve?

CHAPTER EIGHTEEN

HOLY COMPANIONS

WHO'S GOT YOUR SIX?

Some pastors are lone wolves. But being a loner is not conducive to long-term ministry.

The US Army published an article called "Soldiers Helping Soldiers: Battle Buddies Help Each Other During Tough Times." Captain Cameron Albert encourages soldiers to develop friendships that can become lifesavers off the battlefield. "It's really as simple as asking a couple of questions like, 'Are you okay' or 'Do you want to talk about it?'" The article encourages, "We should all have somebody we can confide in. When we have situations that are hard to get through, a buddy can help you come up with ideas and better solutions to the problem. It's a lot easier to talk to somebody you're close with than someone you don't know that well."[1]

My neighbor and good friend Verne served in the US Army in Afghanistan. I asked him about this and he agreed—"You need a fellow soldier who's got your six."

This is true for soldiers in the military as well as soldiers in ministry. Who's got your six? Would someone say of you, "He's got my six?"

Take a look at what researchers say about the problem of isolation in pastoral ministry.

---

1. Russell Sellers, "Soldiers Helping Soldiers: Battle Buddies Help Each Other During Tough Times," Army.mil, September 16, 2010, https://www.army.mil/article/45239/soldiers_helping_soldiers_battle_buddies_help_each_other_during_tough_times.

As of March, 2022, 42 percent of pastors have seriously considered leaving, not just their churches, but the ministry altogether. Three main factors are the immense stress of the job (56 percent), feeling lonely and isolated (43 percent), and current political division affecting their churches (38 percent). Two in five pastors (43 percent) say "I feel lonely and isolated."[2]

The *Journal of Pastoral Care and Counseling* states, "Burnout among clergy is not uncommon and often results from work-related stress stemming from . . . a perceived inability to discuss their personal struggles with others."[3]

Earlier I cited Proeschold-Bell and Byassee, who identify four factors that enable pastors to flourish rather than burn out. Factor number two is "Having a lot of social support,"[4] highlighting the significant role of friends.

The State of Pastors draws this conclusion in a section on Pastors and Friendship: "The correlations between higher friendship satisfaction and lower overall risk [for burnout] make a compelling case for the necessity of genuine friendships among pastors."[5]

Distant as well as recent history led the authors of *Pastoral Friendship: The Forgotten Piece to a Persevering Ministry* to conclude, "Biblical and church history prove that no man will persevere well in pastoral ministry without the grace of friends to walk beside him."[6]

Pastor, would you not only seek the kind of friend, but be the kind of friend whose influence contributes to endurance in ministry? We're going to see an example of this kind of friendship between two key figures in the

---

2. "Pastors Share Top Reasons They've Considered Quitting Ministry in the Past Year," Barna.com, April 27, 2022, https://www.barna.com/research/pastors-quitting-ministry.

3. Webb, *70 (4)*: 266–271.

4. Proeschold-Bell and Byassee, 127ff.

5. Barna Group, *The State of Pastors*, 41.

6. Michael A. G. Haykin, et.al., *Pastoral Friendship: The Forgotten Piece to a Persevering Ministry*, (Christian Focus, 2022), 103.

early spread of the gospel, establishment of churches, and the beginning of the spread of Christianity. Let's survey the development of this relationship chronicled in Luke's writing in Acts and the subsequent letters of Paul.

Prior to chapter 16, the main characters in Acts were Peter and Paul. Luke has been the invisible narrator. In Acts 16, he subtly changes from third person to first person, from "he" and "they" to "we." Luke became part of the story. He joined Paul in his missionary work. I think this relationship became a key factor in Paul's endurance through difficult and demanding ministry.

FROM CASUAL ACQUAINTANCE TO GOSPEL FOCUS

It seems Luke and Paul met in western Asia Minor while Paul waited for the Holy Spirit's direction in the bustling port city of Troas (see Acts 16:1–10). Luke "may have been practicing his profession [as a medical doctor] in Troas at the time, or waiting to be signed on as a ship's doctor."[7] However it happened, the relationship between Paul and Luke first comes into view here. They were in the same place at the same time.

Friendships often begin when circumstances put you together. But the kind of friendship that contributes to long term ministry goes deeper. It grows through mutual involvement in the cause of the gospel.

When Paul was summoned through a vision to take the gospel across the Aegean Sea to Macedonia, he and Luke discussed it. Luke also felt compelled by the need and they stepped through the door of opportunity together. Luke recorded, "And when Paul had seen the vision, immediately we sought to go on into Macedonia, concluding that God had called us to preach the gospel to them" (Acts 16:10).

"Concluding" means collecting facts, evaluating them, and drawing a conclusion.[8] What's especially interesting is that this participle is not sin-

7. F. F. Bruce, *The Book of Acts.* The New International Commentary on the New Testament. (Wm. B. Eerdmans, 1988), 308.

8. William. Arndt, Frederick W. Danker, Walter Bauer, and F. Wilbur Gingrich, *A Greek-English Lexicon of the New Testament and Other Early Christian Literature,* 3rd ed. (University of Chicago Press, 2000), 957.

gular but plural. Paul and his new companion Luke considered together the meaning and importance of Paul's vision. Then the two of them decided that the Lord had called "us" to preach the gospel to the lost in Macedonia!

Their casual acquaintance progressed to a much deeper level. Luke associated himself with Paul in a common cause—the gospel.

For you this might look like meeting a pastor at a regional fellowship or crossing paths because you minister in the same community or a nearby town. Could your casual acquaintance become a gospel-based friendship? You might initiate having coffee and talking about the impact of the gospel in your own lives. Start praying together for gospel work in your churches and in your community. Just think how encouraging it would be to have a friend like that, and praise God if you do!

A pastor I know recounts his proactive pursuit of a mutually encouraging friendship with another pastor. Feeling the need for prayer and accountability for areas of personal character and pastoral wisdom, he contacted a college classmate who pastored in a nearby town. They were acquainted but were not really friends in the usual sense with an already existing natural connection. He had a Subway coupon and invited the other pastor to meet him, where he openly shared his family and ministry concerns, said he desired a relationship with another pastor he could be transparent with and accountable to, and asked if the other pastor would be willing to build this kind of relationship. They began meeting regularly and became close friends who could ask or tell each other anything. Even though ministry assignments have moved them apart geographically, they still talk about once a week, fifteen years later. This pastor says if he had not taken the step of intentionality, the friendship would not have happened.

If you don't have a friend like this, think of the pastors within an hour of you. Consider taking the step of intentionality!

MORE ABOUT GOD'S WILL THAN GOOD TIMES

The newly formed evangelistic team saw immediate fruit when they led Lydia and her family to Christ in the city of Philippi (Acts 16:11–15). Then Paul delivered a slave girl from being demonized, provoking her angry masters to call law enforcement. Things took a bad turn when Paul and Silas were arrested, charged, beaten, and imprisoned in stocks (Acts 16:16–24).

Luke evidently wasn't arrested, possibly because he was a Gentile or was known in the region, but it was a close call. It didn't discourage him from accompanying Paul on future mission adventures. He plunged into danger right alongside the apostle.

Luke is silent about any connection between himself and Paul until about five years later during Paul's third missionary journey. He may have stayed in Macedonia practicing medicine while Paul continued his apostolic travels. Sometimes friendships experience a hiatus, even picking up again after years have passed.

Luke and Paul were reunited when Paul left his meeting with the Ephesian elders. "We . . . set sail" (Acts 21:1), finally arriving at the coastal city of Tyre in Palestine. The disciples there "were telling Paul not to go on to Jerusalem" (Acts 21:4). They made a travel stop in Caesarea, where the prophet Agabus predicted Paul would be arrested in Jerusalem.

Listen to the pathos between Paul and his friends: "When we heard this, we and the people there urged him not to go up to Jerusalem. Then Paul answered, 'What are you doing, weeping and breaking my heart? For I am ready not only to be imprisoned but even to die in Jerusalem for the name of the Lord Jesus.' And since he would not be persuaded, we ceased and said, 'Let the will of the Lord be done'" (Acts 21:12–14).

Remember, "we" includes Luke. Paul's friends were concerned for his safety, but they were committed to God's will. The kind of friendship that encourages endurance wants God's will more than anything. Self-centered friendships are about having a good time together, feeling comfortable, and having fun. Christ-centered friendship is a source of mutual encouragement in doing God's will, even if it's hard for one or both friends.

While I pastored, a man in our church who worked in the medical field started asking me to have lunch with him. We talked about family, day-to-day life, and things we both enjoyed. We played tennis together, and he even helped me learn a slice serve.

Our church went through challenging times that were very stressful. He consistently pursued time with me, asked how I was doing, and prayed for me. He helped me persevere through my hardest days as a pastor. He wasn't just around for the good times. He was much like Paul's medicine practicing friend, sticking with him through hard times in ministry.

It's natural to want a friend like that. I want to encourage you to not only seek but also think about being a friend like that. Is there another pastor you can initiate spending time with and start encouraging and praying for him, acting as a steady presence during hard seasons of ministry? You could make the difference in his perseverance in doing God's will.

ENDURING ROUGH WATERS

Luke and Paul traveled to Jerusalem where the warnings became reality as Paul was attacked by the Jewish leaders, arrested by the Romans, and held in protective custody for two years (see Acts 21:17, 27–24:27). Luke and other comrades were nearby, and Paul's keepers were under orders "that he should be kept in custody but have some liberty, and that none of his friends should be prevented from attending to his needs" (Acts 24:23).

Paul's appeal to Caesar (see Acts 25:11) set the machinery in motion that would finally take him to Rome. Somehow Luke was able to go along for the ride—"it was decided that we should sail for Italy" (Acts 27:1), and what a ride it was! His first-person plural account of their seafaring ordeal reads like *Captains Courageous*.

When Luke and the sailors thought the ship was going to come apart underneath them—"all hope of our being saved was at last abandoned" (Acts 27:20), Paul reassured them all with the message he had received from the "angel of the God to whom I belong and whom I worship . . . 'Do not be afraid, Paul; you must stand before Caesar. And behold, God has granted you all those who sail with you'" (Acts 27:23–24). The ship broke apart on the reef along the coast of Malta, where every soul made it safely to shore. "We were brought safely through," Luke recounts (Acts 28:1). And finally, catching a ride on another ship, "we came into Rome" (Acts 28:16).

Do you wonder if Luke ever thought, "I didn't sign up for *this*!" We all experience rough waters in ministry. Sometimes we don't know if we'll make it through. A friend who sticks close through those hardest of times is a treasure. If you have one, you will appreciate him for the rest of your life.

When you are friends with another pastor who is going through a hard season in church life, you might tend to draw back, not wanting to involve yourself and get tangled up in someone else's church problems—you have enough of your own! Think about sending a quick text, "Hey, I'm here for you. Praying for you and glad to listen if that's what you need." Pastors experience the rough waters of marriage struggles, prodigal children, serious health issues, and so much more. Be the friend who says, "I'm around and will walk through this with you. Just know you have a friend who's praying for you."

Samuel Buell was a pastor in East Hampton, Long Island in the eighteenth century. He wrote of this kind of mutually encouraging relationship: "Friendship . . . affords a sort of life-sustaining power, and virtuous balm, for fainting minds, under over-bearing sorrows, and pours the lustre of day into souls over-clouded with afflictive night."[9]

My wife and I have had dear friends who pressed in close to us when going through the hardest trials of our lives. I've been on the receiving end of this kind of friendship more than the giving end. If you've been blessed by this "life-sustaining power and virtuous balm," give thanks to God and thank your friend. Perhaps you, like me, will pray you can be the source of these blessings for a brother pastor.

DEEPENING OVER TIME

Letters preserve the intimate thoughts of those who write them. Paul's letters from prison mention Luke three times. Evidently, once Luke rejoined Paul and sailed with him to Troas, he remained alongside Paul for the rest of his ministry, to the end of Paul's life.

---

9. Haykin, 60, quoting Samuel Buell's *The Divine Agency Acknowledged in the Death of our Dearest Friends* (J. Parker and W. Weyman, 1757), 10.

He was nearby when Paul wrote the Colossians from prison around 60 AD: "Luke the beloved physician greets you" (Col 4:14). Paul had grown to love him—"the beloved."

About the same time, Paul wrote a very personal letter to his friend Philemon, noting that "Epaphras, my fellow prisoner in Christ Jesus, sends greetings to you, and so do Mark, Aristarchus, Demas, and Luke, my fellow workers" (Phlm 23–24). Though a professional man, not a preacher, Luke truly helped Paul in his gospel work.

Now a long period passes, and seven to eight years later, possibly after release from prison and more evangelistic and church-planting work, Paul is back in Roman prison, knowing the end is near. He writes a final letter, this one to Timothy, his younger associate in ministry. One loyal friend is there: "Luke alone is with me" (2 Tim 4:11).

Paul had grown to love Luke. Luke worked alongside Paul in gospel ministry. He was there for the long haul, whether smooth sailing or stormy waters.

This friendship had deepened with time, as can ours. As we walk together through ordinary life, move from small talk to personal transparency, encourage one another through prayer and the Word, and stick close through the joys and trials of life and ministry, a long-term friendship becomes a treasure of life.

THE FRIEND WHO STICKS CLOSER

As valuable as this kind of friendship is, it never replaces the sustaining presence of our Lord Jesus Christ.

Paul faced a Roman hearing where family and friends could speak in support of the accused. With fierce persecution in the Roman Empire, anyone who showed up at Paul's hearing probably would have been risking their lives. Nonetheless, it seemed he expected someone to be there, but was disappointed.

"At my first defense no one came to stand by me, but all deserted me" (2 Tim 4:16).

However, Paul knew the presence of an unseen but very real friend. "But the Lord stood by me" (2 Tim 4:17).

When even your best friends let you down, One will never leave you or forsake you: "There is a friend who sticks closer than a brother" (Prov 18:24).

Luke was not just a minor New Testament character. He went on to write a detailed narrative of Jesus's life known as the Gospel According to Luke, as well as the authoritative history of Christianity's birth, the book of Acts. These two books together comprise a larger word count than all the letters written by the apostle Paul!

Truly, "The friendship of Luke and Paul was the dynamo that powered the church's growth in its first generation. That was God's providential purpose in bringing them together, because Paul and Luke together accomplished what they could never have done separately. This is the power of friendship in God's plan."[10]

Friendship still has a place in God's plan. I hope the example of Luke and Paul will encourage you to cultivate friendships that help you and others endure in gospel ministry.

---

10. Scott Hahn, "How Luke and Paul's Friendship Affects Us," Angelusnews. com, October 3, 2023. https://angelusnews.com/voices/luke-paul-friendship-hahn/.

REFLECT AND DISCUSS

1. How does this quote impact you? "No man will persevere well in pastoral ministry without the grace of friends to walk beside him."

2. How does the example of Luke's friendship with Paul impact you?

3. Are there steps you should take toward developing one or more mutually encouraging friendships? What will you do?

Part 5

RECOVERY AND FINAL PRAYER

BASIC ACTIONS FOR RECOVERING PERSONAL HEALTH

If you or someone else thinks your personal health is suffering, I encourage you to block out a few hours or even half a day to walk through this chapter. Or you could work through it on a personal retreat.

Approach it prayerfully. Ask God to give you wisdom and the courage to be honest with yourself and others. Journal your thoughts, including the concerns you have, options you can consider, Scripture that comes to mind, and steps you should take in the near future. You may also want to ask your wife or a friend to read over this chapter and share with you what stands out to them.

HONESTLY EVALUATE

You can start on this yourself, but I encourage you to involve a few other people, such as your wife, a pastor friend, or other confidante. Start by stating your ideal priorities as a Christian man, a husband, a father, a neighbor, and a pastor. Then compare how you spend most of your time with these priorities. How well do they align? Look over your schedule for the past six months. Do your time commitments include the practices that cultivate and protect your spiritual, relational, mental, and physical health? How is your state of mind? Are you often discouraged, resentful, or withdrawn? Would you describe yourself or would others describe you as joyful?

PROACTIVELY ENLIST HELP

Schedule a routine medical screening. Your doctor will help you assess your physical health and advise you on steps needed to improve. Set up a time to meet with a biblical counselor or ministry coach. This might be for your personal struggles, your marriage or family, or your ministry. If you need legal or financial counsel, seek out the professionals who can advise you. Don't flounder on your own. Be humble enough to allow others to help you.

TAKE TIME AWAY

The retreat I recommended in chapter 14 may be what you need right now, not for planning, but for personal renewal. Get away and commune with God. It will help you regain an objective view of life and ministry.

REMEMBER YOUR ROLE AND YOUR LIMITATIONS

There are circumstances you can't change. There are people you can't change. There are conflicts you can't resolve. You can't turn a church around, grow a church, or fix all of a church's problems by yourself. Review the primary responsibilities of a pastor. Own what you can do, and honestly acknowledge what you can't do.

DETERMINE YOUR PRESENT ROLE, RESPONSIBILITIES, AND PRIORITIES AND PURSUE THEM

Ask and answer, "What should I be doing here, now? What has God called me here to do? How do my gifts fit the stage of growth this church is in?"

HAVE CONSTRUCTIVE CONVERSATIONS WITH YOUR CHURCH LEADERS ABOUT YOUR PLAN FOR SPIRITUAL AND PHYSICAL WELLNESS

Be honest with your team about where you are in your personal health. You may find it helpful to ask your fellow pastors, elders, deacon chairman, or deacons to read this book. Discuss the areas you think need attention and reasonable steps you can take with their support.

DETERMINE WHEN IT IS TIME TO STEP AWAY

Hard circumstances or personal discouragement don't by themselves warrant resigning your ministry. But if the idea of concluding your ministry where you are and being assigned by the Chief Shepherd to another flock stays on your mind, you should prayerfully evaluate it. The most helpful resource I know of for carefully determining whether it is time for you to change ministries is *Before You Move* by John R. Cionca. I've used it for two major ministry moves. It walks you through assessing factors related to you as a pastor and factors related to the condition of the church. I highly recommend following the steps in this book if you are thinking about leaving your current place of ministry.

MAKE A COMMITMENT

Would you be willing right now to take a few minutes to formulate a commitment to steward your personal life for the purpose of glorifying God and sustaining long-term ministry? If this necessitates pursuing recovery, include in your commitment the actions you've identified from this chapter. Acknowledge your commitment to God in prayer. Then make a list and, with God's enabling strength, start being a healthy pastor.

CHAPTER NINETEEN

REFLECT AND DISCUSS

1. Do you need to take steps to recover any areas of personal health? What does your spouse think? What do other leaders in your ministry think?

2. Will you commit, with God's help, to steward your personal life to glorify God and sustain long-term ministry?

CHAPTER TWENTY
MY PRAYER FOR YOU

Thank you, pastor friend, for allowing me to speak into your life through this book. When I transitioned from pastoring to teaching, I resolved to be a friend to men in ministry. I have benefited from encouragers and mentors, and now I hope to fill these roles for others. This book is one of the products of that burden. I want to end with a focus on prayer for personal health in all the areas we have discussed.

The ideas I have shared are based on the truth that God is interested in more than just your spiritual life and your ministry work. God is concerned about your entire being, and you are a steward of both the material and immaterial components of who you are. Third John 2, which I presented in chapter 2, is evidence of this: "Beloved, I pray that all may go well with you and that you may be in good health, as it goes well with your soul." John prayed for Gaius to thrive both physically and spiritually.

ANOTHER MODEL PRAYER

Another biblical prayer that reflects God's interest in you as a whole person is 1 Thessalonians 5:23: "Now may the God of peace himself sanctify you completely, and may your whole spirit and soul and body be kept blameless at the coming of our Lord Jesus Christ." This is Paul's prayer for the Thessalonians as he concludes his letter to them. We can rightfully pray in a similar way. Let me highlight key ideas in this prayer that guide us in petitioning God in behalf of ourselves and others.

"The God of peace" describes God as the source of peace. Peace can refer to harmony between individuals. It also corresponds to the Hebrew word *shalom*, meaning a state of well-being, including health on every level. Paul calls on "the God characterized by peace in his nature, who gladly bestows it also."[1]

God is the ultimate source of your welfare, health, and well-being. Peace with God is yours in Christ (see Rom 5:1). The peace of God is yours in Christ also (see Phil 4:7). This peace includes, not only relational harmony with God, but the welfare, health, and well-being that God is able to provide in your daily life. This is not a guarantee that you are exempt from illnesses, financial setbacks, or disrupting events in your life. It secures for you an inner stability and freedom from anxiety and provides an underlying foundation for cultivating well-being on every level.

The primary request in this prayer is that God would "sanctify you completely" (1 Thess 5:23 NKJV)—fully accomplish His sovereign purpose of setting you apart for His glory and progressively developing you toward Christlikeness. Notice the object of God's sanctifying work—"your whole spirit and soul and body" (v. 23). Again we see that God's work in our lives intersects, not only our spiritual being, but our physical being as well. I've emphasized throughout this book that you glorify God by stewarding your personal life, spiritual as well as physical, for long term ministry. Here Paul prayed that God would be actively involved in growing them to bring Him glory with their whole person.

I was impacted recently by this statement relating the truth of the resurrection to the value God places on our whole being: "God made the whole man and the whole man is important. The doctrine of the bodily resurrection of the dead is not an old-fashioned thing. It tells us that God loves the

---

1. A. T. Robertson, *Word Pictures in the New Testament, The Epistles of Paul*, vol. IV (Broadman Press, 1933), 38.

whole man and the whole man is important."[2] Our physical bodies were created by God, bring glory to God, and will be reformulated by God with the capacity to inhabit and enjoy eternity. We can and should glorify Him with our whole lives, physical and immaterial, now and we will serve Him in our glorified bodies forever.

Paul continued his prayer, asking that as a result of God's activity they would "be kept blameless at the coming of our Lord Jesus Christ" (v. 23). This is a "prayer for the consecration of both body and soul."[3] Peter recorded a specific promise that pastors will one day be personally rewarded by the Chief Shepherd Himself: "And when the Chief Shepherd appears, you will receive the unfading crown of glory" (1 Pet 5:4). Both in Paul's prayer and in Peter's promise there is an eschatological focus. This long view motivates us for complete dedication to God in present life and ministry.

Notice the words "be kept" (1 Thess 5:23). This Greek verb is in the passive voice and means "to cause a state, condition, or activity to continue . . . for a definite purpose or suitable time."[4] God has a life-long purpose for you that He is perpetuating. Do you ever wonder if you're going to make it? Be assured the God who is growing you is also committed to completing His work. Rest in the truth that He is bearing you up, carrying you along, and will enable you to persevere.

Paul followed his prayer with this hope-imparting promise: "He who calls you is faithful; he will surely do it" (1 Thess 5:24). Maintaining personal health for long-term ministry does not rely solely on your plans, resolve, or self-discipline. God is the only one who is completely trustworthy, and you can rely on Him. Declare your dependence on Him daily, especially through difficult times.

---

2. Francis A. Schaeffer, *Escape from Reason* (Inter-Varsity Press, 1968), 28.

3. Robertson, *Word Pictures in the New Testament*, 38.

4. Arndt, 1002.

PRAYING FOR YOU

Father, I pray now for my pastor friends. Together we thank you for showing us mercy, enabling us, counting us faithful, and putting us in the ministry. We are grateful you have placed each of us where we can shepherd your flock.

You know our weaknesses, faults, and limitations. All you ask is that we faithfully steward what has been entrusted to us.

Please help my pastor friends to rest when it is time to rest, work when it is time to work, and take pleasure in all you have richly provided for us to enjoy.

Impart wisdom for establishing priorities and managing time. Channel the needed volume and variety of grace when they are discouraged, disappointed, and fatigued.

Temper like steel their resolve to protect their purity and guard their integrity all their days.

May their marriages thrive and their friendships deepen.

Enrich their communion with you. May they exult in worshiping you. May they link their identity to you. May they derive their sufficiency from you.

Guide them to identify and implement practices that are most needed.

Energize them to change. Motivate them to persevere.

We live out our lives and labor in our ministries for you. We look forward to the day when we will together meet before you, receive rewards from you, and together praise and thank you, for the One who is worthy is you.

In our Savior's name,

Amen.

www.ingramcontent.com/pod-product-compliance
Lightning Source LLC
Chambersburg PA
CBHW031504120626
46545CB00005B/1749